INSINUATIONS

INSINUATIONS

∼

JACK DANN

An Autobiography

2010

This autobiography was commissioned by Gale Research Inc.
for the *Contemporary Authors Series* 263. Portions of this work
were first published in different form as "Sparks in the Dark" in
Contemporary Authors Autobiography Series, 1994 ("Sparks in the
Dark", by Jack Dann. Copyright © 1994 by Jack Dann) and "A Few
Sparks in the Dark" in Starship, November 1982 ("A Few Sparks
in the Dark", by Jack Dann, copyright © 1982 by Jack Dann).

ISBN
978-1-906301-63-7
978-1-906301-64-4 (signed edition)

Design and Layout by Aaron Leis.
Printed in England by the MPG Biddles Group.

PS Publishing Ltd
Grosvenor House
1 New Road
Hornsea, HU18 1PG
England
editor@pspublishing.co.uk
www.pspublishing.co.uk

The author would like to thank the following people for their support, aid, and inspiration:

Caren Bohrman, Paul Brandon, Norm and Paddy Broberg, Susan Casper, Peter and Nicky Crowther, Lorne Dann, Ellen Datlow, Barbara Delaplace, Terry Dowling, Gardner Dozois, Harlan Ellison, Andrew Enstice, Keith Ferrell, Greg Frost, William Gibson, Nick Gevers, Joe and Gay Haldeman, Merrilee Heifetz, James Patrick Kelly, John Kessel, Charles and Betty Ann Kochis, Mark and Lillian Levy, Joe Lindsley, Patsy LoBrutto and Mary Greene, Barry N. Malzberg, George R.R. Martin, the generous folk at *The Mirror Newspaper*, Anne McCaffrey, Steve Paulsen, Kim Stanley Robinson, Randy Russell, Pamela Sargent, Lucius Shepard, Mark Shirrefs, Robert Silverberg, Nick Stathopoulos, Michael Swanwick, Dena Taylor, Bob and Karen Van Kleeck, Albert White, George Zebrowski, and my beautiful partner Janeen.

INSINUATIONS

For Mitch...
who's certainly on this speeding, paint-faded bus.

July 7th, 2007: The present of things future.

This autobiography has become a collaboration . . . a collaboration with two vaguely familiar past selves who call themselves Jack Dann. They tried to live flat out and scoop up every jot and tittle of life's joys and experience; and, of course, they also managed to step, one clubfoot in front of the other, through the inevitable miasma of disappointment, loss, and grief.

I began this autobiography in 1981, and it was published in shorter form in a magazine called *Starship* and a volume called *Literary Masters*, edited by Jeffrey M. Elliot. I was thirty-six years old, a young genre/literary Turk submerged in the writer's life, in the craft and culture and society of writers. I had been seduced by the idea of being a writer. I wanted to sit on the shoulders of giants, insinuate myself into the generational conversation of great literature, be remembered; and although I knew about death and the needle-sharp finiteness of life, although I had almost died, although I had lost friends and felt most of the adult emotions, life was still a great, tree-lined, winding highway with no discernable emotional end. And there was little separation between living and writing, being married and writing, being a parent and writing, being a son, brother, friend, or, in some cases, an enemy.

I called the first incarnation of this autobiography "A Few Sparks in the Dark" because that was—and is—how memories appear to me. My past has always seemed to be labyrinths of darkness broken only by incandescent flashes of memory, by neon fluorescences of events and dreamtime imaginings that have shaped and continue to shape me. And, yes, I've always had the niggling suspicion that I've also shaped and reshaped my memories to conform to those subtly shifting myths, stories, archetypes, epics, and fables that I've imagined to be my unique personal history. I create memory, and memory creates me (or me's) until it becomes difficult, if not impossible, to separate the truth from the . . . truth.

In 1993 I was asked to write an autobiography for the *Contemporary Authors Autobiography* series, which I finished in 1994. I used the framework of the original autobiography and shortened the title to "Sparks in the Dark". I was forty-nine; and in my midlife summer, I had profoundly changed the course of my life. My old and dear friend George R.R. Martin used to refer to me as "the hermit of Binghamton" because I was so rooted in upstate New York that I would rarely attend functions in such outré and faraway places as Manhattan or Los Angeles. I was—and am—an introvert, a loner, who has chronic feverish episodes of extroversion.

Yet in 1994 I found myself on the other side of the world:

I finished "Sparks in the Dark" in Australia and was also putting the finishing touches to *The Memory Cathedral*, my Leonardo da Vinci novel, which became my best-known work, the book that allowed an unsure, egocentric wannabe to call himself a bestselling writer. I had spent six years researching the Renaissance and the Middle Ages and had discovered Saint Augustine's "present of things past", "present of things present", and "present of things future". So I thought I would literally turn "A Few Sparks in the Dark" into an autobiography told by two selves, for I had originally described remembered events in the present tense to try to capture that sense of numinal "presentness" that seems to characterize memory, as if all the events in deep memory have the same weight and valence and are somehow simultaneous. I wanted to tell the story of my life as . . . story.

But my forty-nine year old self imagined that he was in Augustine's present of things present and writing in the first person past and present tense about Augustine's present of things past. That left my thirty-six year old self in the safe and secure present of things past. The sixty-two year old Jack Dann writing/speaking to you now is—from the perspective of his younger two selves who contributed to this story—caught in the present of things future. My two other selves left me in a bit of a quandary. How do I integrate their future memories into this autobiography and cue the reader as to which self is telling which story? My other selves dated some sections, while others were left to flow dream-like, like memory itself.

I think all I can do as a collaborator with the past is to insinuate myself once again into my own story, become a few more sparks in the dark simultaneity of memory. In this present of the future, I am writing in the guest bedroom of our little farm at the southernmost tip of Australia. When I pause to think and dream, I can gaze out the window at the Southern Ocean and the dinosaur shape called Wilson's Promontory. An eleven-month old tricolor Beagle called Bertie sleeps and dreams beagle-dreams beside me.

Perhaps memory, like fiction, is a waking dream.

If so, it's good to be able to dream some of my story once again . . .

∾

It's September 10th, 1993, and I'm in my office on Ackley Avenue in Johnson City, New York. I'm working in the family home, in the same room that was once my bedroom, and I gaze out the same windows where as a child I glimpsed the nighttime reflections of ghosts and twisted spirit faces. It's early afternoon, and the sun pours in, oak leaves move in green shadows against my neighbor's yellow house; and for this bright instant, I can almost believe that nothing has changed.

Yet everything has changed . . . everything has changed since I sat down in my old office on Main Street to write this autobiography twelve years ago . . . everything has changed in the last four months . . . yes, even in the last week.

In 1987 I moved into a pre-Civil War Greek Revival house with an acre of land and a pond, all in the city limits of Binghamton, New York. I moved with my wife and stepson. My stepson is now twenty-two and on his own. My wife is still in the house, but I am not. I've finally turned from the past. I expect to be out of the country by December. New love, new flowerings of possibility.

Let the future call me a liar.

It's March 29th, 1994. Autumn in Australia. The trees in the park near my partner Janeen's home in Melbourne are just beginning to turn to rose and that fall yellow I remember from so many autumns in Binghamton, when the leaves seemed to be turning into sunshine itself. But it also feels like summer; and as I sit in the garden, sipping tea, writing, and watching the goldfish in the pond feeding on the remains of my breakfast toast, I marvel at how I came to be here in the Antipodes, so far away from the familiar places I once loved.

I type away on my laptop computer, writing this autobiography that has become as recursive as memory, that is still shifting wildly from past to present, to what Saint Augustine called the three times: the present of things past, the present of things present, and the present of things future.

Even I have figured out that it's only a matter of perspective.

~

I've just sat down in a high-ceilinged, wood-paneled country church in Greene, New York. Cold winter light floods through stained glass windows depicting the trials and tribulations of Christ. The pastor blows into his hands and begins his memorial service for Jean Lindsley, a woman I've known for thirty-five years. Her husband Joe sits in the front pew, his long white hair gauzy in the light. Sitting beside my wife Jeanne in the pew ahead of me are Bob and Karen Van Kleeck, two of my dearest friends. I tap them on the shoulders to let them know I'm here, and then we're all standing, Karen loudly praying, for she knows the verses by heart. Suddenly, everyone is embracing. Bob leans over and hugs me, as does Karen. I kiss Karen, then take Jeanne's hand, squeezing it, and kiss her lightly on the cheek. Then Jeanne is sitting beside me, asking for tissues, and for all the world we look as we've always looked: two people who have kept hearth and home together for themselves and their friends. Now another friend has passed away, as if she had always been but a memory, a sweet, poignant metaphor for our marriage.

Then we're all standing toe to heel in the obligatory receiving line in the church social room, which is fitted out with folding chairs and long tables covered with plastic table cloths. Platters of veggies and dip alternate with platters of ham and turkey; the smell of coffee permeates the room. I hug Joe's children, and then Joe and I embrace. I'm crying, crying for the loss of old friends, for all the sweet full memories we've had, for the poor times when we'd get together over bean stew and listen to jazz at Joe's box of a home in the country. "You're doing better with all of this than *I* am," I say to him.

Joe pulls away and grins at me. "I've had more practice."

~

I haven't seen Joe. He went on the road to sell his oils and watercolors in art shows and work out how he could live his life alone. I had once given him my copy of Jean Dutourd's *Pluche*, a book about an artist living the life of art . . . alone; little did I know that in his last years, Joe would, indeed, become Pluche. But he was supposed to be back in town before I left again for Australia. I was supposed to call him. We were going to have bean soup and listen to jazz for old time's sake. I was going to introduce him to Janeen Webb, my new partner.

As I sit in the jumbo jet, looking out the window into the flat darkness of sky and ocean, my knees pressed against the back of the seat in front of me, I can smell his stew.

And I remember . . .

~

It's 1969. I'm twenty-four years old and have sold two collaborative short stories to Ejler Jakobsson, editor of *If Magazine*; neither one has appeared yet. It is a warm, dry summer day, a wonderful day, full of sun and possibility. I am visiting Anne McCaffrey at her home in Sea Cliff, New York. She has a grand old Victorian house with a kitchen on the fourth floor and enough cats padding across the landings and up and down the stairs to satisfy even a cat lady. I've gotten lost in that house before.

I'm sitting in Annie's tiny office on the first floor. Away from the noise. Paperbacks on narrowly spaced shelves cover the walls. The room is dark, almost mysterious, but secure. Anne sits behind her desk and looks at a row of books beside her. She stares hard at them, as if trying to think out the answer to a question. I imagine that if she finds the answer, she will never return to this tiny room again.

"These books are mine, Tawny Lion," she says to me. "It's as if every year is on this bookshelf. One day you'll be counting the years of your life by the number of books you've written. And that's what you end up with, a row of books, the years of your life."

Although it's a magical time of my life—everything bright and compacted—Annie has just come through a bad marriage. She is a tall, large-boned woman with a shock of white hair. She's Irish and used to be an opera singer. She always seems to know when I'm in need of a home cooked meal and some positive reinforcement. She is also the secretary of the Science Fiction Writers of America, an organization I've just joined.

I'm living in Brooklyn, New York, and trying to write and go to St. John's Law School at the same time.

I guess I'm in love with Anne McCaffrey.

It's 1965 and I have a private room in Norwalk Hospital in Connecticut. I'm connected to the bright, flat world of the hospital by plastic tubes—one breathes cold oxygen into my left nostril, another passes into my right nostril and down my throat into my stomach; one feeds me intravenously, another draws my urine. About fifteen student nurses are having a party in my room. It's my birthday. I've suffered a relapse, and my lung collapsed. I have acute peritonitis; none of the antibiotics I've been given seem to be working. Beside me on a moveable table are a philosophy textbook and a copy of Hemingway's *A Moveable Feast*. I put my hand on the books. I'm too sick to read, but I need them there. My nurse Rosie sits beside me and eats a piece of cake.

I wish for another shot of Demerol. I cannot conceive of being without pain. Without the drug, it seems that there is nothing else. The drug represents cold and dream-hallucination, not surcease of pain.

The books. I promise myself that if I survive this, I will do something worthwhile. Perhaps become a nurse; too late for me to become a doctor. I make a deal with God, even though I do not believe in Him. If I live, I promise Him, I'll do something with my life, take chances. I pat the books beside me.

Three weeks before, I had been in coma. My temperature had been one hundred and four degrees for some time.

Right now I think of ice hills and blue music and moveable feasts.

I'm riding in the back seat of a rented yellow car in the winter of 1978. The countryside is covered with new snow; the road is slippery. We're somewhere between Binghamton and Greene, New York, on our way to visit Joe Lindsley and his wife Jean who are waiting for us in a redneck bar where they feature country rock bands.

One of my dearest friends is driving the car. This is the first time we've seen each other in seven or eight years. The government has just given him a new name and identity. There's a lot of blood under our bridges. We were going to be artists together. We were going to become engineers and found a company called SEA—Submerged Experiments in Agriculture. That was in high school. We even had an engineer working with us. But we went our own ways, and finally found each other again.

I'm having trouble calling him by his new name, which he insists upon. We talk about Joe, who is a framer and used to work in a frame shop on Main Street in Binghamton. When we were fifteen and used to come into the shop to buy art supplies, he would talk to us for hours about painting, literature, current events, philosophy, whatever he was interested in at the time. He always had stacks of books in the back room, books on painting technique, books containing drawings and paintings by old masters, history books, and, of course, modern and classical literature. He especially loved science fiction. Most of his books he borrowed from the library. But everything was new to us. What the structured school system had tried to extinguish, or at least divert, Joe rekindled every week.

My friend has a new wife, who is beautiful and has a mane of thick red hair. I nickname her The Lion.

There is a lot of laughter and fast-talking in this car. Trying to catch up on two lives in a few hours. My friend puts his arm over the back of his seat, looks at me in the rear-view mirror, and says, "Jackie, do you remember when we were in high school and one day instead of going home we went walking around Clinton Street? We were walking across the bridge and you said you were going to be a writer. You just knew that. Nothing was going to stop you. And you walked along, swinging your arms, saying over and over, 'I'm a writer, I'm a writer, I'm a writer.'"

Surprised, I say, "No." I try to remember, but it's all gone.

It's February 4th, 1981, and I'm in my office on Main Street in Johnson City, the same Main Street that runs through Binghamton where Joe Lindsley worked as a framer and where he later opened his own shop. I sit here trying to construct—or reconstruct, I should say—my past.

Anne McCaffrey was right. As I look through my stories and books, I can remember writing each one. They're the pegs upon which hangs my past. These books are my memory.

It's March 29th, 1994, and my books, papers, files, photographs are unavailable to me now, for I've left them all behind. As I look at the pages I wrote thirteen years ago, I realize that memories are small bright fictions, approximations of reality filtered through the various lenses of experience. It's all basically true, I tell myself, but the filter of experience changes, twists, and creates so many truths out of the original remembrance. In 1981 I was a writer. Now I just write. Being a writer doesn't seem very important. The work, the process, is important.

But so is chewing up every moment as if I were nineteen . . . so is living for and in the moment. This is the moment. There's not enough time left to be complacent. It's taken me twenty years to learn to put words on paper, only to discover that I've got to begin all over again. I had an idea for a novel about a writer who misses out on his life because he's always involved in a book or a project. His children grow up before he has time to notice. And when he does, it's all gone; the years turn his life to paper.

That's the straight line extrapolation of this writer's life from the perspective of February 4th, 1981. And it's mostly true.

But it didn't quite work out that way . . .

When I was in the hospital for a four month period, I had such a high fever that I developed a mild amnesia. My memory has holes in it. It's as if that time in the hospital was so intense that it burned entire areas of my memory and lit others with an almost numinous light. Indeed, I feel like Vonnegut's Billy Pilgrim, snapping back and forth in time from one incident to another. That's the visceral sense I have of it, anyway.

That night when I went to Greene with my friend was one of discovery. My friend talked, probed, and suddenly I found myself remembering. The memories came back to me with the strength of hallucination. Like Billy Pilgrim, I went back and forth in time as if dreaming reality. And even now I keep discovering, remembering, as the overpowering intensity of my time in the hospital begins to wane just a bit.

But even with a perfectly clear memory, I would have to sneak up on my past, take note when a familiar sight or smell jogs loose an old memory. My past must be constantly snared; it would be a hunt, even without the burns of amnesia.

So now I'll begin in the conventional way. What follows was written in February, 1981 . . . before everything had changed.

I was born in 1945 in Johnson City, New York, about two blocks away from my present office. Although I've spent quite a bit of time away from this area, it has always been my home; and I returned for the kinds of emotional layering and correspondences that I find only here. It is as if there is a corresponding map of Johnson City and Binghamton in my mind, only this map is one of space and time—a grid, so to speak. I remember this same building where I now have my office as it was when I was a child—the building hasn't changed, but as I have, I see it differently now. And yet I have that visceral sensation that the other "me's" caught in those beads of time that I perceive as the past, are still here. And I remember, or rather see, the world as I saw it then. In a way, it's like living in an excavation, and one's life becomes an archaeological dig.

In the course of a day, I pass by old buildings where I used to live and places where I used to play. I see ghosts everywhere as I pass back and forth through the years, and many of those ghosts are myself. I remember walking up and down Main Street with Gardner Dozois, one of my closest friends, and experience once again that sensation of compacted experience, of being alive in an open-ended way: the time of the twenties when, as Harlan Ellison might say, we live at the top of our lungs.

Johnson City is a sleepy town that lies between Binghamton and Endicott on the northern side of the Susquehanna River. (Taken together, the populations of "The Triple Cities" are almost as large as that of Syracuse, our northern neighbor.) It is located in a valley, which has almost constant cloud cover, and lies in the midst of some of the most beautiful country I've ever seen. I'm in love with this little piece of the world, as can be attested by the alien scenarios of my novel *Starhiker*, many of which are really descriptions or exaggerations of upstate New York countryside.

I feel a strong sympathy for the way Andrew Wyeth painted Kuerner's farm in Pennsylvania for twenty years, going back to the same place over and over again, and always finding the new in the old, a world in microcosm. That is somewhat the way I feel about the whole Binghamton area, and upstate New York in general. Ray Lafferty once wrote that certain parts of the country, the old lands, have ghosts, the layering of generations. (He wrote this as fiction, of course, and as memory isn't strong on this, I may be garbling what he wrote.)

For me, this land has its ghosts and layerings.

And I find it amusing and ironic that at the time when I was asked to write this autobiography, my work was changing shape, as I've discovered my home to be my "Kuerner's".

But this work is really for the future, which holds a novel, already begun, entitled *Counting Coup*.

Of course, it was another "me", caught in a bead of time perceived as the present, who wrote that. Like me, he was blind to all but the past. He would not have been surprised to discover that Binghamton would continue to inform and give form to his work in such stories as "Fairy Tale", "Playing the Game" (with Gardner Dozois), "Slow Dancing with Jesus" (with Gardner Dozois), "A Cold Day in the Mesozoic", "Reunion", "Bad Medicine", "Tattoos", "The Apotheosis of Isaac Rosen" (with Jeanne Van Buren Dann), "Visitors", "Blues and the Abstract

Truth" (with Barry N. Malzberg), "Kaddish", "Voices", and "The Extra".

He finished his contemporary novel *Counting Coup* and sold it for a rather large advance for the time to Bluejay Books, which then went out of business. The advance went toward the down payment on the Cutler House, a three-story Greek Revival where he would live and work for five years. But all that has been seen of that work are the excerpts "Bad Medicine", which was a Nebula finalist, and "Counting Coup", published in an anthology about American Indians entitled *Tales from the Great Turtle*. As one New York editor said, *Counting Coup* has become an unpublished underground classic.

Being blind to the future is most certainly a blessing.

From the perspective of years and the distance of some 9,000 miles, I see the person who began this autobiography thirteen years ago in an entirely different light. He was trapped in his own version of Kuerner's farm, and if his life had not exploded, if he had not been thrown out of it, as if from a cannon, he would still be there now living in the very small and very secure spaces of his own construction. But when he wrote that, life was determinate rather than synchronistic; he could plan and extrapolate, and find things amusing and ironic. He could afford to be smug.

His father had not died.

He had not yet lost so many friends to cancer.

He had not fallen in love.

He had not felt enough pain.

He had not yet discovered how to live in the moment.

And he didn't know that the compacted times, the times of being most alive, were ahead of him.

It's October, 1988, and I'm standing in my father's private room in Lourdes Hospital in Binghamton. I stand beside my mother, and we stare dumbly at my father, who has passed away only minutes ago. He died quickly, in my mother's arms, of an aneurysm. Images pass through my mind as I look at my father, who seems to be merely asleep, oblivious to my mother's soft, choking cries. And I remember when nurses wheeled him toward me on a stretcher years earlier. He had just had surgery for a melanoma and looked like a corpse. Yet he was mumbling something, chanting it over and over. I leaned toward him to hear "They can't kill Murray Dann . . . they can't kill Murray Dann."

I remember when he had discovered that one of his lungs had to be removed. He called from Florida and insisted that I fly down and drive him north to Binghamton. I told him that he needed surgery as soon as possible and should fly home. He refused, and so I caught a plane into summer, and drove him from Florida to Binghamton. We talked of last things, of guilt and mistakes, and I absolved him as best I could, told him that no one deserves to carry such guilt, that that was absolution itself.

And we drove eighty-five miles an hour up I-95 in his big gold Lincoln with the windows open and the air-conditioning turned to high. We talked and drank from his hip flask that was in the shape of a demon and flew towards the darkness together.

Images projected on my dead father lying in his hospital bed. My mother leaves me alone with him, and I pace back and forth across the room, talking, trying to squeeze it all in, even though he's dead, even though he can't hear. But I can't stop talking. All the words left unsaid. Now said in the cotton silence of that room. Now I can leave him, but when I reach the waiting room, Mother insists on taking a last look. I go back with her, lest she be alone with the dead, and there I discover something about the nature of the soul, for now I see only a dead, plastic form, empty.

My father had left.

∾

The story "Voices", published in the August 1991 issue of *Omni Magazine*, was born out of that experience.

~

My father was an attorney. He married his childhood sweetheart, worked in a bank, and studied law at night at St. John's Law School located on Schermerhorn Street in Brooklyn—I was to study law at the same school, with the same teachers. After passing the Bar, he moved to Johnson City and bought the white, hacienda-style stucco house I grew up in. My mother lives there now. It is full of the ghosts of better times.

I grew up with science fiction books, as my father was an avid reader and kept his science fiction collection in my bedroom. I used to look at the lurid covers and dream about them before I was old enough to read them. I can still remember the Hannes Bok cover of the first science fiction book I ever read: *The Green Man of Graypec* by Festus Pragnell. As a child, I stayed to myself. My books became my closest friends.

I went to public school until I was fourteen. I did my share of fighting, as I was one of the few Jews in the area. The fighting prepared me for the military school I was to attend for two years. With the exception of art classes, I found school boring and began to get into trouble with school authorities and finally the police. My parents suggested a private school, and I jumped at the chance for supposed freedom. I chose a military school because their promotional booklet looked glamorous, containing photographs of young men skiing, playing war, wearing uniforms with swords, and dancing with pretty young ladies in grand ballrooms.

The slogan of The Manlius Military Academy, located just outside of Syracuse, New York, was "Manners Maketh Man". I never did discover the logic of that, but it was the school code. Manlius was supposed to be the stepping-stone school for West Point, which was probably true, as many private schools have special relations with particular colleges. Manlius boasted that its varsity football team played the West Point frosh, which we did, every year—an excuse to take a bus ride and smoke all the cigarettes our lungs could stand.

Like West Point, Manlius was at that time a strong hazing school, and was really two worlds. We were, of course, regulated by adults, our instructors and military people. We went to classes, did ROTC every day, went to church in formation like penguins on Sunday, and dutifully wrote our parents. That was the apparent world. But the hour by hour life of the new student, the newboy, was controlled by older students. In truth, children ruled a world of children, and being children, punishment for an infraction was severe.

My roommates Crocker and Palomar are taking a smoke in the woods by the old water tower. I'd like a cigarette right now, but I've got to wait in the hall and make sure no one goes into the lavatory, which is catercorner to my room.

One of the newboys is getting a GI shower; I can imagine how he's being scrubbed from head to foot with wire brushes and lye soap. But I can hardly hear the screaming over the radio noise. My radio. It's playing "Duke of Earl", my favorite song. My face is still bleeding from a pimple I had to cut with a razor blade. I remind myself to call Mom and Dad tonight.

It's Sunday afternoon, and A Company dormitory is almost deserted.

Then with a "halloo", they drag the newboy out of the john. He's not screaming or fighting, just whimpering. But Jesus Christ he's bleeding everywhere but from his balls. The other guys are all excited. They're laughing and dancing around. One is even stupid enough to be carrying a wire brush into the hallway. And another one has a hard-on.

I duck back into my room, and everyone else gets out of the hall. Sergeant Wells Morton, who has a room across the hall from mine, hasn't seen nor heard a thing. He's been working on an overdue paper. I know that newboy is still out there, but all I can do is imagine him standing in the hall, bleeding like a pig.

Well, he should have taken a goddamned bath once in a while.

The school is closed now. I went back for a look some years ago, went back in the middle of winter when the snow drifts were four feet deep. The red brick buildings seemed to be rising out of nowhere, as if seen in a dream, and once again slipping back, I saw myself marching again, as if inside the snow, and a fistful of those beads of time played before me. And I remembered. I cried with nostalgia—nostalgia for a time and a place I had hated. Now it had been suddenly transformed into "the good times", but only when I wasn't snapping back and forth, only when I could look through the past with thirty-five year old eyes.

I returned to Manlius because I had (and still have) a novel in mind about the school. An old school chum had told me that the school had been closed because of a homosexual murder. If, indeed, what he said was true, I knew one of the professors involved.

And I remember a time when the entire football team was kicked out of school a week before graduation because of a homosexual incident. I can still remember the excitement shuddering through the various company dormitories.

I leaf through my old yearbooks and find photographs of myself standing with the other boys of my company. Once again I discover that those are photographs of little boys, and yet I remember a world that was very different from anything the eye of a camera could see.

The world I remember was something like Salinger's *Catcher in the Rye*; in fact, the campus he describes was very much like that of Manlius. But that world was also like the movie *If*, or *Lord of the Flies*, which I read after getting out of the hospital in 1965.

I remember those times as being hard-edged and cold as a GI shower.

I'm working on a novel entitled *Extra Duty*. It's about that boy who stood in the hall while the newboy was being roughed-up in the shower. Only this time he witnesses a homosexual murder.

~

And now I'm forty-nine, rereading old material written in earnest; and separating the truth from the fiction. *Extra Duty* was a white lie, for I wasn't working on that novel, except to think about it once in a while. But I had learned from my friend and collaborator George Zebrowski how to fool myself into being a writer from one week to the next. George has often acted as my own personal Dale Carnegie, although in these hard days of the 90's, we have often reversed those roles.

So I thought about a novel entitled *Extra Duty* and stuffed it right into my biography as work-in-progress. There, another book. You *are* making progress, Jack.

Perhaps I shouldn't be so hard on my old self, as thinking about a story is really only a hair's-breath away from producing it. Easy to write this now, as I sit here in the sun in Melbourne with a fax beside me that came in at 4:00 AM. I just sold a new novel about the Civil War, entitled *The Silent*, to my editor at Bantam Books for more money than I would have dreamed possible in the early days.

As I think about it, *The Silent* owes much to my Manlius experience. And, who knows, *Extra Duty* may yet be written. George called me last night to tell me he had worked out a plot for a novella cobbled out of an outline for an old novel of mine, titled *The Mindcasters*.

After all, writers resurrect the dead as a matter of course.

Like Salinger's protagonist, I kept running away from school and was finally taken out by my parents. I was offered officer's rank and the run of the school if I would stay because the school was using me as an example of what they could do with a boy. When I entered Manlius, I failed four courses. When I left, I was on high honor role.

I came back to Johnson City, but went to school in the next town, where I had some friends I had met at Manlius. It was at Binghamton Central High School that I met the man mentioned in the early flashback. He tried to overdose on aspirins, of all things, and then we lost touch. Later, Joe Lindsley told me he was importing wild animals into this country for zoos.

But I'm jumping ahead, for Joe told me that when I was in college.

Truth be told, almost all of that high school time is lost to me. Perhaps it will come back.

When I try to remember, as I'm doing now in 1994, I'm reminded of skin-diving in the lakes in upstate New York where visibility at best is around five feet. Everything is gauzy, hazy, lit in a nimbus. I hold my breath and dive to about fifty feet, as the blood pulses in my head and the gray, gauzy water world becomes even more two-dimensional. And there, in the flat, constricting haze, I encounter the unpredictable: a silvery school of fish suddenly reflecting and refracting all over me like aluminum shards inside the polished tube of a kaleidoscope. For that instant, I'm overwhelmed, but only for an instant, for I need oxygen more than anything else . . .

I remember attending my thirtieth high school reunion at the IBM Country Club on a hill in Endicott, New York. I remember the expansive rooms and buffet, the corkboards covered with yearbook photographs, the balloons and streamers, and vaguely familiar middle-aged strangers laughing and shouting and embracing, as if trying to crawl back into the discarded snakeskins of their adolescence. The men are balding . . . the women wide and puffy and lacquered. I remember shaking hands and wondering who these people are who seem to know me so well.

A man and a woman stand before me, drinks in hand, both dressed casually; old hippies just going to seed. But obviously successful. "Hey, Jack, we came down from LA just for this. We wanted to see what had happened to you. So you *did* become a writer. Well, you crazy sonovabitch, you certainly influenced us in the early days."

I smile and nod and cannot for the life of me remember who they are.

Silvery fish swimming around me in the gauzy light.

Feeling pressure in my lungs for oxygen, I excuse myself.

I'm at a party in the convention suite of a science fiction convention. I can't remember the year or the city, for all convention parties seem the same, as if time has collapsed in between them, leaving one continuous party in which the participants only become older. I'm sitting on the floor with Lucius Shepard, James Patrick Kelly, John Kessel, and Gardner Dozois. We're all fairly drunk, and Jim looks at Gardner and me and says, "I was

reading you when I was in high school. I wanted to be like you
guys . . . you were always out there, on the barricades, right in
front. You held on to your integrity."

How could he have been reading me in high school? He can't
be much younger than me . . . can he? And John agrees with
him. Indeed, we were right out there, doing our thing, snubbing
our noses at being "commercial", starving our stupid asses off.
But we'd kept our integrity.

Indeed . . .

At the mention of "integrity", Lucius begins pouring beer into
my empty shoes.

Such is the reward of holding out for integrity on the barricades of science fiction.

～

I went to Hofstra College in 1964 for two reasons: I was interested in becoming an actor, and Hofstra had a good reputation;
and at that time Hofstra had no dormitories. After Manlius, I had
sworn I would never live in a dorm again.

When I was taking my entrance examinations in 1963 at
Hofstra, which is located in Hempstead, Long Island, I heard
someone in the large room shout my name. I turned around
to see my friend Charlie Kochis taking the same examination.
Charlie and I had gone to Manlius together, had been best of
friends.

We roomed together for most of the two years that I attended
Hofstra, and later, when everything had fallen in for him, he
stayed with me in Johnson City and now lives in Binghamton.
He was with me in 1965 when I had an appendicitis attack and
took me to Meadowbrook Hospital. I was put in a ward with
about five other men who had been wounded during a shooting.
One lent me his radio, and I remember a good feeling of fellow-
ship. I was examined about twenty times by different doctors,

students, I supposed, as I was asked the same questions over and over again.

Charlie phoned my mother who, when she found out that I was staying in a ward in a welfare hospital, took me to a private hospital in Oyster Bay, Long Island. She had the best intentions. But neither of us knew that the hospital was unaccredited, had no access to a blood bank, and was involved in illegal abortions for the rich. Some years after I left, the hospital was closed by the state.

I had a beautiful room overlooking the ocean. I remember a cross hanging on the white wall opposite the window. I was operated on, a routine operation, and then everything became like a dream. My stomach was full, I was in agony. My private nurse, a man who had once been a professional boxer, told my parents that they'd best get me out of this hospital. He felt I would probably be left to die. My parents called Dr. Ed Rem, an old family friend, who examined me and ordered an ambulance immediately.

I was taken to Norwalk Hospital in Connecticut, where I had three emergency operations. Although I had originally gone into the hospital with appendicitis, I had developed peritonitis. The doctor in the Oyster Bay Hospital refused to admit that anything was really wrong, even though my stomach was obviously distended.

I spent four months in Norwalk Hospital on a terminal floor, where I watched my friends die, one by one. I saw the best and the worst of people, met with death, and saw myself reflected in the flames, saw myself as I really was—and have been trying to change ever since.

Patients on a terminal floor live in a world unto themselves. They have their own ways of communication, their own ways of coping and helping each other. The nurses and doctors and families that walked in and out of our rooms lived in another world. They never saw us as we were, as we saw ourselves. In the microcosm of a terminal floor some of the patients play out the last of their lives heroically, just as others beg and plead and whimper.

I remember a man in the room across the hall from me. He cried and screamed day and night, trying to make deals with God and the angels, begging for another chance. He was in agony, and nothing seemed to help him. He had lost most of his stomach because of ulcers. I remember my own pain, and I remember hating that voice across the hall, wishing it to cease. I imagined that the man was a baby, an ancient babe, and I wished it dead.

Later, after the man died or left the floor, I wanted another chance to feel right about him. In the hot logic of my fever dreams, he had died because I had wished him dead, because I thought wrong thoughts.

And I understood that that whimpering thing was me, and that I won't allow myself to forget.

I couldn't integrate those experiences into my fiction until 1977 when I wrote "Camps", which appeared in the May 1979 issue of *The Magazine of Fantasy & Science Fiction*. It is a story about a dying boy in a hospital who has recurring dreams that he is in a concentration camp. His nurse, who had been one of the first women to enter the camps at the end of the Second World War, discovers that his dreams are real. He is dreaming about the camp she had entered, and his life in the present, in the hospital, depends on a past known only to his nurse. She must guide him through the past. And now, as I write this, I understand why my protagonist Stephen flashes back and forth through time, from hospital to concentration camp. Those sections that take place in the hospital are based on my own experiences. Some are exaggerated, of course, and others didn't happen. But I was Stephen, hooked into machines, dreaming Demerol dreams of ice fields and blue hells.

And yes, again for an instant, I'm still Stephen.

∾

It's disconcerting to look back on one's work and see that, indeed, it is of a piece. Much of my work is about the nature of time and the waking to consciousness, and there is a sequence of short stories that seek to "testify" to the fact of the Holocaust that begins with "Camps". Gardner Dozois and I wrote a story, entitled "Down Among the Dead Men", which raised hackles among critics and writers alike. It was about an inmate in the camps who was a vampire. Other stories followed: "Tea", "Kaddish", and the science fiction novelette "Jumping the Road", which was the cover story for the October 1992 issue of *Isaac Asimov's Science Fiction Magazine*. The themes of time, consciousness, memory, the camps, and hospitals recur in my work like the objects of worship floating just below the surface of the ocean in "Kaddish". My story "Visitors", which first appeared in the October 1987 issue of *Isaac Asimov's Science Fiction Magazine*, was about a dying boy whose hospital room becomes crowded with the ghosts of dead patients.

My nurse's name was Rosie, and she was twenty years my senior. I remember sitting on a bed with her in a motel room filled with family and friends. I had just left the hospital, and we were celebrating. And I remember how I felt when they wheeled me out of the hospital, remember crying at the sight of sky and trees and children, at the sound of cars and crickets. In tears I demanded to drive, and I drove that long black Cadillac as if I wished to be back in the hospital again.

I felt I had to squeeze life, as if to death.

Rosie and I sat on the bed while everyone else drank and talked. We cried and held each other. She had gotten too involved, had slipped into the world of the patient, and I had caught her. We knew each other intimately, as well as lovers (although the most we had ever done was to hold hands), knew each other as well as parents can know children, as friends can know friends.

She would always look the other way when I was naked.

I was in love with Rosie, still am. Right now I remember her coming into my room at 6:00 AM and knocking something or another to the floor to announce her arrival. I remember . . .

I received a letter from Rosie several months after I left Connecticut. She told me that one of my closest friends, a patient, had died. He was an engineer and had a lovely wife and mistress who would visit me on alternate days, just as they visited him. He was in his late forties, had white hair—as white as Annie's— and he had a particularly painful form of cancer.

One night, just about the time when he would walk over to my room for a hand of pinochle, I heard a crash in the hall. Rosie came back with the news: he had been given enough sedatives to put a horse to sleep, yet he tried to walk to my room. By rights, she said, he shouldn't have been able to move. I knew why he did it: he didn't want me to think that anything was wrong.

I remember a policeman down the hall whom I never saw. He had been shot several times. He had five kids. Every night he sent his nurse over to find out how I was doing. We talked to each other through our nurses, sent messages back and forth every night, and as I had relapses and recovered and was delirious, I imagined that I was talking with him and his family. He died, and the nurses closed all the doors, as they always did.

And we all knew him, even though no one ever saw him.

We also knew the man who had swallowed four quarts of motor oil and was six hours on the dialysis machine.

We knew him, we knew them all.

∾

I never heard from Rose after that. I wrote her one letter, but she never replied. I think about her every week or so. It is becoming easier to think about that time.

~

I'm standing in Barry Malzberg's living room. The walls are covered with books. Two couches and a coffee table seem to fill up the room. Across the room and to my right are the glass doors of Barry's office.

It is 1975 and summer. Barry and George Zebrowski and I have just driven back from New Jersey, where we attended a dreadful party at Roger Elwood's home. Half of the people at the party were writers and half were members of his church. We rode up and back in Barry's Cadillac. The party was so uncomfortable that Barry and I kept sneaking out to the car to nip at a bottle of bourbon that he kept in the glove compartment for just such emergencies.

George, who is in another room talking to Joyce, Barry's wife, has been quite optimistic all day. He and Barry have been arguing about the fate of science fiction, the growing book market, and hardcover vs. paperback books. George has been telling Barry that he, Barry, has hurt his career because of his approach to the field, *because* of his pessimism. Barry became angry and left the room, then returned, only to pace.

Now he is standing beside me. He is well over six feet tall and is dressed in a white shirt with a tab collar, the kind worn during the sixties that pushed out the knot of the necktie. He is wearing a black tie and jacket; he has not fastened the little tabs under the tie. He seems to loom beside me, a great black bird.

"You think you're like George," he whispers, as if George is in the room and might hear. "You think that by being diligent and producing a body of good work it will somehow work out." He pauses to fit a cigarette into a holder, and I wonder if the pause is for effect. "You wait and see, you'll feel differently. There's too much darkness in you, you won't be able to delude yourself much longer. You'll see, you're like me . . . "

I nod and feel the man's power, his unique charisma. It's as if the darkness he spoke of, which he represents, has become suddenly palpable. Yet I can see a row of his books across the room.

He *has* succeeded. How can he feel he's a failure?

~

Such questions, questions that would be absolutely obvious to anyone but a writer, had to wait nineteen years for an answer. It's not the number of books or the quality of the work. It's about having a life.

It's far too easy to forget that there is life other than printed words and deadlines and conventions and awards, and far greater failures than bad books, or books that don't sell. And I'm embarrassed to admit that it took so long for me to figure that out.

I think the expression is "Get a life".

~

I returned home from the hospital in the late summer of 1965. I had become institutionalized, in that when it was time for me to leave the hospital, I wanted to stay. In fact, I managed to stay with Rosie an extra few weeks by feigning illness.

I remember an old acquaintance who had spent most of his life in jail. He used to talk about prison as if it were a social club. He knew he was going back; he was only out for a while.

I understand that now, just as I understand Barry . . .

~

I still had the drainage tubes in my abdomen, and they remained in place for another month. I could not face going back to school, could not face any responsibility, but finally I became bored and entered SUNY at Binghamton. It was there, in my senior year, that I met George Zebrowski and Pam Sargent. I met them in an astronomy class.

The year was 1967. Later that year I met Josiane Mueller, who was Pamela's roommate. I remember going to that apartment. Pam was in the living room, sitting at a table and working on a philosophy paper. Her boyfriend George lived in the apartment below, I believe (memory suddenly becomes clouded), and he walked into the apartment while Josiane was getting ready for our date. George, who is about five foot five inches tall with long blond hair and a square, boyish face, immediately told me that he was a science fiction writer. He spoke very well and was dressed more like a professor than a student—in those days denim was the student's uniform.

George seemed to know everything about everything. He took me over to his apartment and showed me his stereo system, upon which he played only classical music. Although he had not yet been published, except in amateur fan magazines, he began talking about what it took to be a writer. Then he showed me a fanzine that *he* had published.

We discussed reviving his magazine, and suddenly I knew I was going to become a writer. If George could be a writer, so could I. In the next few months, I spent almost all my time with George. He would read to me for hours from books about writing. George loved to teach, and I listened to everything he had to read. It didn't matter that George was almost as green as I was about the craft of fiction. He knew where to look to find things out, and he believed so strongly in himself, that I did, too.

And then we were writing. Every night we would sit across from each other at his living room table and type. It was a wonderful, novel time. Everything seemed possible. I was reading everything put before me. I was a sponge, as malleable as I've ever been—and I hope will ever be—in my life. Everything seemed new to me—philosophy, science, literature.

I did the first drafts for several stories. George then reworked, plotted, and did the clean draft. I'll admit that my memory is not clear about much of that time, but I remember that the idea of writing, of working with words, seemed magical to me. When I was a child, I thought that characters in books awakened when you opened the book and went back to sleep when you closed it. But they were *real*. And some of that stayed with me then. I felt that for the first time I was dipping into the stuff of life, and like a boy coming into puberty, I was quite overwhelmed by what seemed to be happening inside me.

Although George always assumed the role of teacher, I began to teach myself to write. I remember memorizing whole passages from Fowles's *The French Lieutenant's Woman* and Kosinski's *The Painted Bird*. I tried to make their very words and rhythms my own.

Of course, I could not write—or do what I considered to be writing. The stories I wrote with George were finished (a major accomplishment for any writer), and he sold two of our earliest stories by giving them to an editor at a science fiction convention.

But I did not feel like a writer. I could not even begin to express my thoughts and sensations on paper. Everything I wrote seemed amateurish, which, of course, it was. But I was determined to learn the craft, and craft became everything. I thought only of learning how to write, how to make the words correspond to my thoughts. I began to listen and learned how to speak properly. Everything became form, everything was thought of as craft of fiction.

I graduated from college in 1967 with a BA, although I didn't receive my diploma until 1968. I did not attend the ceremonies; I felt removed from the whole college experience. I had made few friends, and have, regrettably, lost touch with those years, except for writing.

George and Pam became my family. But I was immature and still emotionally weakened from my time in the hospital. I let myself slide into the role of child, and George and Pam became surrogate parents.

I was to regret that slide later, although as I think about it now, I realize there was nothing any of us could have done. I feel that that "me" was very different from the man I am now, although, quite frankly, I can't help but like that past self. He was a mongrel, an amusing puppy. But I also realize he had quite the potential to turn into a dangerous animal (which some might argue he had!).

I just received a fax from Pam Sargent. My connections to business and old friends are now fax, e-mail, and telephone. Although *I* don't have any real sense that I'm living on the other side of the world, most of my friends feel those 9,000 miles that separate us.

George called yesterday, and I had to keep reminding him that he was spending 70¢ a minute to schmooze. But he told me it didn't matter, much, as he'd just gotten off the phone with Arthur Clarke, who lives in Sri Lanka. He'd already run up the phone bill. What was a few more dollars? George, Pam, and I had made it through the long years of silence, but we are more like family than friends; and now, once again, we keep each other safe, for the 1990s are both the best and the worst of times.

I guess I just had to grow up.

Or grow old . . .

Insinuating myself back into my story, my life.

My old selves certainly understood the value of perspective and reflection, but in 1994, I had no real concept of growing old; old age was just some demarcation sign I'd approach on that wide winding highway. Growing old was what everyone did . . . eventually; but not me, not yet. I was still in the thick of it.

But surely, some things had changed . . .

I remember walking down some sun-lit street in Binghamton, New York with my step-son Jody, remember watching three pretty young women approaching us, smiling, sending out those ancient sexual igneous rays from their wide and clear eyes, those rays of thrumming, electrical, telepathic connection that so often used to vibrate through me. The ancients believed that the eyes were the windows of the soul; those "come hither" looks were certainly (or at least certainly metaphorically) powered and propelled by that ancient, frangible energy. As those young women approached us, I suddenly realized that I couldn't feel the energy, couldn't feel the connection . . . and those definite come hither looks were being directed by those beautiful ray gun eyes at Jody, *not* at his middle-aged step-father. Ah, epiphany.

Now at sixty-two, feeling young yet wondering why my father's aging face keeps staring balefully at me in the morning mirror, I try to take it in stride when lovely and lonely gray-haired old ladies of approximately my age or older smile as they pass me by on the streets of Melbourne or on the main street of my village near the sea.

I can still remember that thrilling, constant sexual thrumming of youth, those concentrated rays, those windows of the soul; but they've now become soft noises and faint reflections . . . for the most part.

Age does present some few, albeit juvenile compensations.

I can get away with playing with my dream-images, becoming an aging James Dean when those blue-haired ladies smile and giggle, wearing sunglasses at dusk, shirt collars turned up for warmth and 50s cool, enjoying the bitter-sweet cocaine sensation of being the oldest kid in the neighborhood. What other people think becomes about as important as wearing gumboots or engineer boots when digging in the garden.

35

Yet I can remember when it all changed, when one world set like an autumn sun and another world revealed itself . . .

Dusk, a languid Australian summer night in 2005.

I'm sitting in Norm and Paddy Broberg's huge, high-ceilinged living room that overlooks Wilson's Promontory and the cold dark waters of Bass Strait. The room is filled with rows of folding chairs and movement: people taking their seats, greeting neighbors, the pleasant susurration and buzz of chit-chat, the familiar faces of retirees I see occasionally in town or at the markets. A Steinway grand piano has been moved to center stage, so to speak. Norm's filigreed pots—produced with an alchemy of craft deserving of inclusion in *Ripley's Believe It or Not*—line shelves and cabinets, and paintings lure the eye away from the magnificent views of hillock and water framed in another wall . . . of glass. Norm is a potter and painter; Paddy is a musician. And this room—right down to the acoustics—was built for concerts.

Paddy tells us to please be seated and introduces a young, award-winning classical pianist. She then graciously steps away so the callow-looking young man can explain what he is going to play. My wife Janeen sits beside me. I can smell the sandwiches in the formal dining room behind me. People shift in their chairs, someone nods to me, I hear the water steaming in the kitchen.

The pianist plays . . . brilliantly.

Minutes pass into a liquid sort of timelessness, and I'm reminded of lucid dreaming, one of my tools for working out difficult plot problems. Rhythm, music is tidal, it inhales, exhales. Breathing deeply, regularly, music in, music out until a trilling of keys, sharp and crisp, breaks my reverie; and I realize with a cold, numbing shock—as if I've been thrown overboard into some Antarctic sea—that almost everyone here is . . . old.

Not old to my present self when he is in thinking, rational mode; but old to those restless other selves that continue to inhabit his psyche.

Here is a sea of gray, a winter of white. Here be wrinkles and lines and the ever sharpening marks of crows' feet. And as my thoughts stream and steam, I'm suddenly caught in some comically cruel stream-of-consciousness passage of Joyce's *A Portrait of the Artist as a Young Man* or Henry Roth's *Call It Sleep*.

I'm old, we're all old, they're retired, gray, don't trust anyone over thirty, prostatitis, constipation, irritable bowel syndrome, ingrown toenails, diarrhea, cholesterol, hernias, arthritis, Dad died of an aneurysm, Mom died of cancer, skin cancer, lung cancer, brain cancer, and the concert is over, the pianist is bowing and

I'm hungry, thinking of those sandwiches. Janeen touches my hand. Red hair frames her beautiful, regal face.

Knowing, tilted green eyes.

And I quickly pass through one world into another.

Revelation, fear, mortality fade away into the stinging sounds of clapping hands and the impatient rustling of clothing. I look at Janeen and smile, gloating. I may be gray, a silvery shadow of my old selves, but I sure as hell know how to rob the cradle . . .

George called yesterday.

He and Pam have been going through my old papers that are stored in their cellar. They wish I were there. Just like old times. Except he and Pam now have a large, book-filled home in Albany, New York. Binghamton is now mostly a construction of memory; when I go back home in real time, I find a city where I have to use the GPS navigation system on my rental car to get from one almost familiar place to another.

George, ever blessedly didactic, talks on and on, politics, books, and philosophy. He is still altruistically crusading for good causes, still on fire as he was when we were in our twenties.

I guess we just burn at different temperatures.

~

It is interesting how many faces we show to those around us. When Gardner Dozois first met me, he thought I was nothing but a street hood, a hard-faced, pimply kid who couldn't talk well and wore his hair greased back into a DA.

I don't remember looking quite that bad.

In the spring of 1969 I moved to New York to study law at St. John's Law School. My father had convinced me that I needed something to "fall back on" in case writing didn't work out—and I had just about had my fill of washing windows, distributing soup, ghost-writing letters for a crazy old lady who thought the FBI was after her, and clerking. I would write in-between times, I told myself.

Although I tried to keep writing, law school took up all my time. I was in an accelerated course. There was no vacation time, but one could finish in two and a half years. Josiane came to New York, and we moved from Brooklyn to Manhattan, to the Lucerne Hotel on 79th Street between Broadway and Amsterdam. We lived in two furnished rooms with a close friend, Don Klisto. But communal life was not for me. My relationships with Josiane and Don were deteriorating, and after witnessing a robbery in the building across the street, Josiane and I moved to Sea Gate, a walled-in village at the very end of Brooklyn.

Most everyone I talked to about Sea Gate considered it to be a very posh area. It was, in fact, very reasonable. We first moved into the one and only sleazy apartment building in the area, but we were right on the beach and even had a tiny, private square of back yard.

I was living there when I received the news that Don Klisto had committed suicide.

Several months later we moved a few blocks away into a charming apartment with two balconies overlooking the ocean and all utilities included for $90.00 a month.

There, within earshot of the constant murmur of the sea, I began to write. I wrote "Whirl Cage" one night in my little apartment—my office was in the hallway. It took four hours and a pack and a half of cigarettes. I sold it to Damon Knight's *Orbit 10*. Damon was editing one of the most influential original anthology series of that time, and its contributors were taking a good portion of the Nebula Awards. The year was 1970, and we were on the tail-end of what's become known as "The New Wave", a period of literary experimentation in science fiction.

When I received Damon's letter of acceptance, it was summer-time again. Calmly, I walked onto the beach—Josiane was at work—and then shouted and ran around, rolled in the sand and chased the seagulls.

I *was* a writer.

I quit law school a few weeks later.

As I reread what my other, somewhat familiar selves have written, as I write interstitially—this feels like just another collaboration; I could just as easily be collaborating on a novel or story or article with Jack C. Haldeman, Gardner Dozois, or Barry N. Malzberg—I keep glancing out the window, staring out at the calm sea hazed by mist and clouds. And I realize that I've always been happy near water, near the sea.

The smell of salt and clean, washed air.

I guess I've come full circle, traveled to the other side of the globe to find another ocean . . . and what might also be called a home of the heart. As I gaze at the sea, I can also see deep green hills and geometric lines of trees. If this crisp winter air wasn't as hard as crystal, enabling me to see details so clearly, I could almost imagine that I was somewhere in Tuscany.

Tuscany, which might be another dream-home of the heart . . .

I'm sitting in the hallway of a hotel at a science fiction convention. I can see the party is in full swing in a room down the hall. The door is open, and fans and writers are filtering in and out. I've had enough to drink so that everything seems pleasantly glazed, and yet I feel a certain clarity, too. It's as if I'm watching a good print of *The Godfather* with its slow timing and deep colors.

Joe Haldeman is sitting beside me. We pass a bottle of Johnnie Walker Red back and forth. Joe has recently sold *Mindbridge* to paperback for a hundred thousand dollars. He talks about Viet Nam, and it's as if I'm caught in his life, in his nightmares. We both share memories we can't live with. Joe takes my hand, grips it strongly, as if to break the bones, and says, "If you keep writing the shit you're writing, you're going to go crazy. You can't dig into that stuff and not go right over the edge."

"If I don't dig into it, I will go crazy," I say, and he lets go of my hand. "That's the only thing keeping me sane."

Joe chuckles as Barry Malzberg comes out of the party suite and sits down beside us.

Barry and I made a deal in the early 80s, the same pact I had made with Don Klisto, may he rest in peace: if either one of us feels like ending it, he *must* call the other. After about a million words of correspondence, Barry and I came, blinking, into the light. We had talked ourselves off the wheel.

I was determined never to make the mistake I had made with Don.

And I suppose that Barry was determined not to make any such mistake with me . . .

∿

But, indeed, I did make that mistake again.

In 1989 I was writing, working nights directing sales for an insurance company, and, as if time was infinitely expandable, I also started a marketing/advertising/public relations firm with Rich Alverson, a quiet, talented loner. I knew nothing about advertising, but I had been doing contract work as a writer for IBM and other companies, so I just assumed (with the ignorance, persistence, optimism, and self-confidence of youth) that a writer could pretty much do anything that involved words. Rich was experienced in computer programming, technical documentation, event management, and the creation and production of corporate video. I could sell ice to Eskimos, to coin a politically incorrect phrase, and so we hung around in corporate lunch rooms, insinuated ourselves into sales meetings, took on any project that came our way, and found our niche in what used to be called corporate communications. Although the corporations had their own public relations and marketing firms, small contractors could always find inside work: newsletters, trade shows, various employee training programs, videos, event management. Rich and I were the company. Two guys in suits with a nice letterhead. When we'd pull in a large contract, we would call in our "distributed network" of professionals, who were usually willing to contract for short-term projects.

In other words, *Alverson & Dann* had a bunch of highly-talented friends: designers, graphic artists, programmers, video technicians, and, of course, writers.

Between working with Rich and directing national telemarketing campaigns for an insurance company—between writing erotic fiction for slick magazines under a pseudonym and writing my own novels and short stories in the wee hours of the morning—I was able to pay the mortgage on my newly-purchased three-story Greek Revival house with about an acre of land and private access to a lake (actually a national wetland) in the center of Binghamton.

Rich and I worked together cheek by jowl and over the months and years became dear friends. Although we had offices downtown, one image is prominent and clear in my memory: Rich's rented house . . . scuffed oak floors, closed blinds and curtains, twilight and gray shadows, empty pizza cartons piled everywhere, well-worn cloth sofas, large record collections, a twenty-seven inch television console, more and more and more pizza cartons, as if he were saving them up to create some sort of amalgamated 1960s pop camp George Segal composition. But his back yard was well-tended, mowed, and large enough for Lady, his pit bull, to run, roam, and play.

Pit bulls have a deserved reputation for being dangerous and inconstant; but Lady was a sweet old thing . . . well, perhaps I misremember; perhaps she was wound as tight as Rich.

Rich and I were doing quite a bit of work for New York State Electric & Gas. Aside from the occasional "big money" contracts (big money only in our terms, of course), we produced, edited, and sometimes ended up writing or rewriting most of their in-house trade magazine. I remember one June deadline. My marriage with Jeanne had fallen apart. I had moved out of the house. I was physically, mentally, emotionally sick with grief. I was an endorphin addict going cold turkey.

I tried to pull myself together by spending a few days in Philadelphia with Gardner Dozois and Susan Casper. I talked and talked and talked. They listened without complaint. I slept fitfully on their couch and patted their cats. Then Rich called to tell me that we had to pull the magazine together.

"I just need another day or two."

"We've got to pull the magazine together," he said, his voice flat, hard, as distant as if he were calling on a bad line from Australia.

He just wasn't going to cut me a break, and I was angry. If the situation were reversed, *I* would have covered for him. Had covered for him.

Only later did I discover that he was angry, too. He was furious with Jeanne for hurting me, and somehow he transformed his love, generosity, friendship, and warmth into cold, unyielding anger and directed it, or deflected it, towards me.

We got the magazine out.

Rich moved to Albany.

I moved to Melbourne.

Two years later, when I was settled in Australia, my mother called to tell me that Rich had asked for my phone number. She didn't feel right about giving it out. Rich asked if I would please call him.

"Here's his phone number, dear . . ."

I *was* going to call. I just needed a little time to pick up the phone.

Rich died of a massive stroke. He was in his mid-forties. He died alone . . . I don't know if Lady was with him, but I can't help but imagine her sniffing around those large, empty rooms piled high with empty pizza boxes. When a mutual friend told me of Rich's death, old memories flooded back, forgotten conversations were suddenly remembered; and something Rich had once said to me echoed in my memory, something dark and ugly dredged up from the mossy undergrowth of my unconscious . . .

When you give up on someone, Jack, you don't threaten. You don't try to do them in. You just walk away. You just erase them from memory. It's as if they never were.

I didn't give up on you, Rich Alverson.

Nor you, Don Klisto . . .

I was just too weak-minded to pick up the fucking phone.

~

I met Gardner Dozois in 1970. George Zebrowski introduced us at a Nebula Awards banquet in New York City, but we didn't say more than a few words to each other. It was obvious that this man who looked like a sixties hippie didn't like me. But several weeks later Annie McCaffrey invited Josiane and me to help collate the *Science Fiction Writers of America Forum*, a newsletter for members of the organization. Of course, she also invited Gardner, as she thought we should become friends.

I was living in Sea Gate at that time, and Gardner was living in a slum on the lower east side of Manhattan.

Gardner has had an important effect on my work and my life. He has been the editor on almost every piece of fiction I've done since "Whirl Cage". We've shared all the times together, the good ones and the bad. In fact, our lives have been so intertwined that I don't quite know where to start, and once started, I'm afraid I would certainly go over deadlines and the amount of words I'm allowed.

Gardner brought me into the Guilford Writers Workshop, which used to meet in Jack C. Haldeman II's four-story Victorian home in Guilford, Baltimore. (Yes, it was in its way like Annie's house in Sea Cliff.) I became a regular member of the group called the Guilford Gafia (nicknamed after "The Milford Mafia", which was what some people were calling Damon Knight's and Kate Wilhelm's Milford Writers Conferences). Our group comprised Jack and Joe Haldeman, George Alec Effinger, Gardner Dozois, Ted White, Tom Monteleone, Robert Thurston, William Nabors, and myself.

Guilfords would last a week-end. Those were some of the most exciting and exhausting worktimes of my life. Lasting friendships were made at the Guilfords. Those workshops were very helpful and important to me. I've been to workshops since, but I don't really get enough out of them any more to go to many, although Gardner and I and Michael Swanwick and Susan Casper tried to revive the old Guilford in 1980 and called it The Philford Writers Workshop. We met twice, and writers such as David Hartwell, Samuel R. Delany, John Ford, James Patrick

Kelly, Timothy Sullivan, Tony Sarowitz, Gregory Frost, and Tom Purdom attended.

I did go to one of Damon and Kate's famous Milford Conferences, which was held in Michigan at Gull Lake. I had gone to visit Gardner for a week-end, and he talked me into going to a convention in Washington and then back to Baltimore for a Guilford that had been scheduled after the convention. And then Gardner and Joe Haldeman talked me into driving to Michigan for the Milford Conference. I had been invited to the conference, but I had no money. Joe and Gardner paid my way, and Damon, if I remember correctly, gave me a break on the room charge when we arrived in Michigan. After a week of workshopping stories, we returned to New York. We were completely exhausted. My week-end visit had turned into a month.

Several months after I sold "Whirl Cage", Josiane decided she wanted to return to Binghamton and go back to school. I left with her in July of 1970 and was once again back home, and writing. I was selling everything I wrote, thanks to editors such as Damon Knight and Michael Moorcock. I took two courses in the graduate school of SUNY at Binghamton, one in Expressionistic art and literature and the other in Decadent art and literature. I had already been influenced by the surrealist movement, especially by artists such as Max Ernst—such influence can be seen in my novel *Junction*. I was quite impressed by the Decadents, especially Joris K. Huysmans's *A Rebours*. My story "Windows" was a homage to Huysmans. But it was the psychologism of the Expressionists that affected me profoundly. One might say that my later work was as much influenced by Expressionists such as Munch as by anyone in the science fiction genre.

Gardner, who was visiting me often, began pushing me to externalize my fiction—the Guilfords had been a great help in clearing up some stylistic problems I was having. But I was becoming too subjective, and my stories were too much about the interplay of my characters' thoughts and too little concerned

45

with the physical world. As George Zebrowski had once described one of my stories: "It's like having your face pulled down onto the paper. Everything feels close-up, as if it's being pushed right at you."

Looking back now at stories such as "Windows", I feel that they were right for their time. They convey a sense of falling, of fluidity, that could not be accomplished with another style. It seems almost ironic to me that I could move so far in the opposite direction that by 1977 I was writing in the cool, objective style of "A Quiet Revolution for Death".

∾

From the perspective of this narrative about the evolution of my style, I am in the present of the future. It's now 1994, and I feel so removed from my old obsessions about style. "A Quiet Revolution for Death" was influenced by Robert Silverberg, who wrote the novella "Born With the Dead", which I would rank with "Death in Venice". But I was still copying, still trying on new suits, so to speak; and it would take years until I found a way of writing that was entirely my own, a way of writing that was not "style" but direction.

However, sitting here in my office as the rain pounds on the roof and the Eucalyptus trees shake in the wind against a two-dimensional gray sky, I am wary of making any pronouncements on my style (or anything else!), lest another "me" in the present of the future read this and shake his head.

But then again, one can't live in fear of one's (future) self.

∾

Another "me", in another present of another future, has just read this and isn't shaking his head. What the hell's wrong with making pronouncements?

46

It's July, 2007, winter in Melbourne. I'm writing this in Janeen's and my two bedroom "bolt-hole" in the city. The apartment is in East Melbourne, a small, leafy, quiet neighborhood divided by the formal 19th century Fitzroy Gardens. It is only a short walk through the gardens—along flower trimmed laneways, past white pergolas and splashing fountains—to the Paris End of Collins Street and central Melbourne. This whole area, with its Italianate townhouses, gothic mansions, and gingerbread fretted apartments reminds me of some dream-like, dreamed-up Bertie Wooster land. I can see an old Silver Shadow parked on the curb beside the Powlett Reserve where golden Gatsby scions and debutants walk their city dogs past the children's playground and tennis courts. A garbage truck creaks and slowly shudders its way down the street, the gear-grinding noise waking me from this odd reverie; and I can't help but smile . . . after all these years, throughout all the hustle, the talking the talk, making money, going broke, and making money, it's *still* all smoke and mirrors. All *maya*, all illusion, and like my grand old Greek Revival, which my friends used to refer to as "the money pit", the bolt-hole in Melbourne and the farm in East Gippsland could all be gone tomorrow. But if I've learned anything, it's to live right in the moment, running headfirst, eyes open or closed, into life as fast as I can; and when I hit that great big wall in the sky, I want to hit it so goddamn hard that there won't be anything left to bury.

That's what I've come to believe. That's what I *still* believe; but right now, this second, it all rings rather hollow.

I call Susan Casper again in Philadelphia.

I've been calling every day . . .

Gardner has just had a quintuple bypass operation. The surgery went well, and he was about to be released: he was packed, ready to go home, and resting in a chair . . . when his eyes rolled back, his heart stopped, and he coded. His stepson (and my godson) Christopher immediately began CPR; Susan called the nurses, and Gardner went back into surgery for a defibrillator implant. Susan

47

told me yesterday that he's fine. He has some shortness of breath, but that's from a few small blood clots in the lungs; he should be out of hospital in a few days.

I haven't been able to talk to him yet.

The phone rings out. There's a clicking, but no answering machine message. The line goes dead.

I'll try again later . . .

April 1994. It's the National Australian Convention, and William Gibson is the guest of honor. We're on the roof of the Southern Cross Hotel beside the swimming pool. In the background are Melbourne's skyscrapers set off against a clear, blue sky. It's April. The sun is hot, and the feel of it on the skin is delicious. Bill and I discuss the hole in the ozone that's right above us while technicians from Public Television set up their equipment. We're going to do "station identifications" for programs we've never seen . . . and probably never will see. Behind us stands a man in plastic *Star Wars* armor. He must be sweating to death, but he doesn't say a word. He's a good media soldier.

As I sit beside Bill, I remember his first novel *Neuromancer*, which took all the awards in 1984. My novel *The Man Who Melted* was on the same Nebula ballot that year. I saw *Neuromancer* as a harbinger, which it was; and the cyberpunk movement, which it started, has become a real element of modern popular culture. As Bill said, "It's bohemia with computers."

"I missed the whole cyberpunk movement. I was writing and researching my da Vinci novel, and when I woke up from the Italian Renaissance six years later, everything had changed."

"I don't know," Bill says. "We always figured you were there."

But I wasn't. I was following my own labyrinth, which had led me from wild literary experimentation to a thousand-page narrative that was the antithesis of post-modernism. Its purpose was to suspend disbelief, to create memory and experience rather than artifacts.

I had hidden myself in the past, in research, in words, in a fabrication that had gained such verisimilitude in my mind that I could quit the present world.

As my first marriage dissolved, so did *The Memory Cathedral* breathe and live and grow.

~

April 12th, 1997, and Janeen and I have taken a weekend vacation in Portsea, a beachside resort in Victoria, Australia. We've booked into a gracious old hotel and are sitting by the pool. It's a cool, sunny day, and businessmen wearing slacks, jeans, polo shirts, and clean white sneakers sip glasses of wine and read *The Weekend Financial Review* and *The Saturday Age*. High-society Toorak matrons wearing uniforms of black Armani and perfectly coiffed bleach blond hair lounge beside their forced-casual men.

Janeen and I sit by ourselves and sip cocktails.

I was up for a luxury weekend, but feel uncomfortable with all the rich wannabes. I retrieve a free copy of *The Age* from the concierge and browse through the arts section. A cursory look at the bestseller list.

The Memory Cathedral is right the hell there: number five!

Fire falls from Heaven, angels sing in perfect harmony, porters scuttle, the sun will shine forever.

I shout "Holy shit" and begin to dance around the pool like a seagull that has just impacted with a plate glass window. Janeen gazes up at me, those beautiful brown-green eyes quizzical. The other hotel guests are no doubt wondering why such a resort of previously good reputation is now catering to the so obviously down-market hoi polloi.

49

By the end of May, *The Memory Cathedral* reached number one.

So there was five minutes of fame, and, of course, the overreaching expectation of more of the same.

But we all know about overreaching expectations . . .

～

July 14th, 2007. 1:30 AM.

I try to reach Gardner again. He is still in the intensive care unit, but Susan is with him, and she has a cell phone. Gardner takes the phone. His voice is craggy and breathy; he is still receiving oxygen.

"So I died and came back."

"I told you you'd make it."

"Well, it's either on or off," Gardner says. "I don't think there is anything else, any kind of life after death. One instant you're conscious. The next you're not. Gone."

"Well, you're here."

"If I wasn't, you'd be writing a eulogy."

"Yeah," I say, remembering . . . remembering.

"I love you, Gardner."

"Love you . . . "

～

Indeed I remembered writing a eulogy for Bob Sheckley, an old bus-mate of mine, who died December 9th, 2005.

I wrote about my bus . . . and Kurt Vonnegut's idea of the *carass*.

A *carass* is your small family of friends who have a special affinity with each other. It's your family of the heart, and like family, you don't choose those in your *carass* . . . somehow, by some strange cosmic iteration, they just seem to come together, are suddenly magically *there*, each one profoundly different from the others, yet each one owning slivers of each other's souls. You might not see them for years or you might correspond with them twelve times a day and see them on Sundays. They aren't just pals. They aren't necessarily even your best friends. You don't always know their intimate details, their resumés, spouses, and toilet habits. What you *do* know is their dreams, for their dreams resonate with your own, with your blood and bone and being. Perhaps it's pheromones, some indigenous soul chemistry that we will isolate in the lab some sunny day. But until then, it can remain part of the invisible weave of magic.

I remember one of those people in my sometimes happy and sometimes unhappy *carass* grabbing my hand at a party in L.A.. Looking daggers into my eyes, he said, "You know I would die for my friends."

I knew what he meant . . . and I knew he meant it.

I think of the disparate group of people in my *carass* as "being on the bus". It's a small bus, and for better or for worse, we're on it together. There are still quite a few people on the bus, although I wouldn't feel comfortable telling you who they are. Some are passionate; some are passive. Some would die for their friends; some would be content simply to console or grieve. I have a lot of other dear friends—friends I love, admire, care for greatly, and enjoy—but they don't share this particular bumpy ride on this particular paint-faded bus.

The passenger list is growing ever smaller: sweet Jenna Felice is gone. Jack C. Haldeman isn't sitting beside me next to the window anymore. I miss Pete McNamara, and where the hell is Norman Talbot, that grand old poet, publisher, and superman tippler?—it's just too quiet. And sonovabitch! Down three seats and across the aisle, Bob Sheckley's seat is now empty.

But I didn't write a eulogy for Jack C. Haldeman, known as Jay to his friends.

No, in December of 2002, I wrote Jay a letter . . .

I had spoken to Jay before he began radiotherapy, and he told me that he was going to try to fight the cancer that was already in his kidneys, liver, lungs, and brain. He knew he couldn't win, but he wanted some quality time to be with his wife, author Barbara Delaplace. I told him that, when the time came, if he wanted to sit on the beach and hang out like in the old days, I'd get myself to Gainesville. He said, "Yeah, I'd like that." That was the last time we spoke. I kept in constant touch with his wife Barbara—I was ready to get that flight from Melbourne to the States—and she kept me abreast of how Jay was faring. As Jay had a very rare form of cancer that wouldn't respond to chemotherapy, he decided to take a chance on a more experimental drug therapy.

It was a gamble, but it just *might* work.

Jay lapsed into coma in the hospital.

For a week Jay's family and friends held vigil. They talked to him, stayed with him, played his favorite music. Barbara told me that no one was sure whether Jay could hear what was being said to him. It was impossible to know.

But I was 10,000 miles away.

So I did what writers do.

I wrote.

Dear Jay,

I asked Barbara if she would read this letter to you, my dear pal. Although I'm far away in terms of distance, I feel as if I'm right in the room with you, with Barbara. You know, you and I never needed to say I love you. It was the groundwork of our relationship, although we did say it, and often.

So this, my dear pal, is a sort of a love letter.

How to say goodbye? We really can't, can we, because we live in each other's hearts. We hold each other in memory, all those younger selves long gone, yet for us they live on, for all the yesterdays seem like only moments past.

We've had times together, haven't we pal, some of the most important times. Remember when we had finished the proposal for *Ghost Dance*? We were sitting around in my old Greek Revival house on Front Street in Binghamton. We were drinking beer. It was four o'clock in the morning, and, thank God, we'd finished the damn thing. The only thing left was to send it to the publishers. And then—I can't remember which one of us it was—we suddenly realized that we'd forgotten the aliens. And the goddamn aliens were the whole point of the book! Remember how we rolled around laughing. We couldn't get up from the floor for at least ten minutes. Couldn't stop laughing.

Jay, the times flicker like a movie before me, all the juicy bits of life that we've shared, all the moments of joy and tears, but mostly joy. Remember when we were working at your house on *High Steel*? I'd come down to visit, and you'd bought that goddamn bottle of Drambuie for me. You kept me drunk for most of the week, and we wrote like maniacs. I remember at one point that I was writing all the science stuff and you were doing all the literary stuff. So, I guess with the help of some good booze, you turned me into a hard science writer.

I remember talking to you on the phone about the climax of *High Steel*. You'd forgotten that *you* wrote the key scene. You sent it to me and I just noodled with it a bit. Well, you called and told me what a terrific job I'd done, that the scene really moved, that you couldn't stop turning the pages; and I kept trying to interrupt you, saying, "Jay, *you* wrote that. Jay, shut up for a second and listen. *You* wrote that."

We worked so well together we forgot where one left off and the other began.

When we talked a few weeks ago, I told you that if you want to sit on the beach together, I'd get on a plane and we'd do just that . . . sit in the sun and talk about the old times, relive the bits, be together. Yet here I am in Melbourne, and yet—Jay, I remember with such numinal clarity when I came to visit you in Gainesville. How many years ago? Was 1980s, I think. We went out to the beach. It was a perfect day, not a cloud in the sky, warm, but not sticky; and we walked, and you told me how much you loved the sea and the beach; and on that day, I, too, fell in love with it. To this day, I find sublime contentment on the beach. I don't live far from the ocean here in Melbourne, and every time I walk along the shore, whether here or in Newcastle on Redhead Beach, every time I'm at the beach I think of you, my pal. I think of that bright day and the joy of being young and being with you. I can still smell the salt in the air.

And here it is, two days away from New Year's, and I remember New Year's in Terrytown, all of us together—you, Joe[1] and Gay[2], Gargy[3] and Sue[4], Rusty[5], Piglet[6], Mom and Dad Haldeman, and I remember the signs Mom used to put on the fridge: HI, JACK, THERE'S FOOD INSIDE ME. I think I lived in your folks' fridge during those holidays. And I remember the mynah bird that mimicked Ma Haldeman's voice. Who would have thought that twenty years later, I'd live in a place where there'd be mynahs in the back yard?

I long for those times, for that sense of family, for Guilfords, where you, old pal, provided the foundation for those workshops. I remember you reading stories half the night with us, then workshopping, and then going out and working a full-time job.

Although I don't know how to say good-bye, my sweet pal and brother, there are a few things I want to say. I want you to know that Barbara will have support from all of us. I want you to know that she'll be fine, that we'll take care of her, just as you

1   Joe Haldeman   3   Gardner Dozois   5   Rusty Hevlen
2   Gay Haldeman   4   Susan Casper   6   George Alec Effinger

and she have always been there for us. I want you to soar with a light heart my dear friend, my old companion. I want you to know that everything will be fine for Barbara, and that all of us will love and take care of each other.

I want you to know that now you can be free, truly and finally free, free to fly, to make this passage; and in our time, in God's time, my pal, we'll all follow. I wish you the clearest skies and warm days. I wish you the smell of salt and the cool purling of the seas. I wish you the joy of being free, of flying and floating; and you'll be here, in our hearts, every single day.

My brother, wait for me on the other side where the winds are soft. Wait for me on the beach where there's no darkness.

Fare thee well, my dearest friend. Fly free. And let me say it this one last time:

I love you, Jay . . . I love you, my pal.

—JACK

~

Barbara told me that she read my letter several times to Jay. Perhaps he heard . . . and perhaps—perhaps in times of splintering grief—all reductive atheists like me pray to the creator(s) of quarks and atoms for Heaven and successions of sunny days after death.

Jack C. Haldeman II died at 1:45 PM, January 1st, 2002.

~

In 1972 I was living alone in Binghamton in a little garret apartment with tallow-yellow walls, odd-angled ceilings, and a space heater with a window through which one could watch the gas fire. Josiane and I had broken up.

In August I sold my first anthology, *Wandering Stars*, to Harper & Row. Gardner had sold them an anthology entitled *A Day in the Life*. It was unusual for young writers who had not yet written novels to be able to sell anthologies, and we began to be touted as the new, young breed of anthologists—I would later try to downplay the editorial side of my career in favor of writing. I was teaching writing and science fiction courses at the local community college to help make ends meet. I met Joanna Russ, who had become an instructor at SUNY at Binghamton, and we became good friends. Joanna is a tall, imposing looking woman. Like Barry, she seemed almost destined to be a loner, no matter how many people might be around her. But we had an almost intuitive sort of communication. I remember taking a trip with her to Ithaca, where she used to teach at Cornell, and being introduced to one of her friends as someone who doesn't need to be introduced. I'd swear that during that time Joanna and I were almost telepathic; we each seemed to know what the other was thinking.

Through Joanna, I got a teaching job at Cornell for that summer. It was ironic, as the English department at SUNY Binghamton was making it difficult for me to get into their graduate program. Since I couldn't get into the university as a student, I went to Cornell and taught—a singularly interesting and exciting experience.

In January of 1972 I sold a story called "I'm with you in Rockland". It is a story about masculine symbols of potency; it is, of course, about impotence. Tom Scortia bought the story for an anthology on sexual themes entitled *Strange Bedfellows*. I remember staying up all night with Gardner Dozois after a Guilford workshop. We worked over a first draft of "Rockland", Gardner piecing together the sections, diagramming, talking about the rhythm of the story as if it were a poem. That was a watershed story for me because the narrative voice was distant, foreshadowing some of the cooler stories such as "A Quiet Revolution for Death" and "Camps".

I had also written the first draft of a novella entitled "Junction", which I later turned into a novel. "Junction" brought me my first critical notice. The story was complex and dealt with some rather unusual philosophic concepts, even for science fiction. It was a Nebula Award finalist in 1973—Gardner and I were competing in the same category that year—and has gained a sort of underground reputation.

It is with nostalgia that I remember writing "Junction". I was writing about fifteen to twenty pages a day, and every night I would drive over to George Zebrowski and Pam Sargent's apartment, and they would read what I had written that day as if it were a serial. I felt at that time that I could keep up the pace forever.

Gardner and I were visiting each other often, and each time Gardner came to Binghamton we would drive to Milford to see Damon Knight and Kate Wilhelm. We never gave Damon and Kate any notice; we would just arrive and stay the weekend. They had an old mansion called "The Anchorage", where the Milford Writers Conferences used to be held. Gardner and I were gypsies then, living in Binghamton and New York, always traveling from one workshop, convention, or friend's home to another.

It was with sadness that I recently learned that "The Anchorage" had burned to the ground.

That same year, 1973, I edited an anthology entitled *Faster Than Light* with George Zebrowski. I sold a story to Harlan Ellison's *Last Dangerous Visions* entitled "The Carbon Dreamer". It was about an old man who witnesses a murder on the beach in Sea Gate. And that year I met a young woman named Marcia.

It was also that year that Joanna Russ and I had an argument that ruptured our friendship. I still regret that I have not been able to repair that.

And into 1974. Gardner and I sold an anthology, *Future Power*, to Random House; and I sold a novel to Bobbs Merrill entitled *Starhiker*. I sold the novel on sample chapter and outline. I was, as usual, in need of money, and I felt that I could write an adventure novel quickly. Actually, I boasted that I could do it in two months. Gardner, knowing better, chuckled when I told him what I was going to do. He was right, of course. I soon became bored trying to follow a standard adventure plotline, so I kept injecting new ideas to make it interesting for me. Before I knew it, I was writing more than an adventure novel.

At the time, I thought that *Starhiker* would be my second book, as I had been working on a novel version of "Junction" while I was teaching at Cornell. But it was *Starhiker* that I finished first. When it appeared in 1977, the reviews were mixed. People seemed either to hate it or love it. The book was finally published by Harper & Row. I had bought it back from Bobbs because I felt that they weren't pushing the books in their science fiction line.

Harper loved the book, but it didn't have any promotion budget, and it disappeared like a shell thrown into the sea.

It is 1971, and I'm with Gardner Dozois in my parents' home. It is a square stucco house, all white except for a great blue front door and black trim along the edge of the roof. It's summertime and Gardner and I are sitting on my bed in my old room, which has been kept just as it was when I left home. I can see into the back yard through the window over my desk. I look at the sunken garden and the broken white fountain and remember getting drunk in the back yard last night with Gardner and the woman we're both in love with. It was a silly night, Gardner singing old rock and roll songs, all of us taking a walk down Ackley Avenue, then coming back and trying to turn on the spotlights for the fountain.

"We should make a pact," Gardner says. He's sitting beside my ebony black night table and leaning against the headboard of the bed. He has long blond hair, a light-complected face, and a thin curly beard. His eyes are pale blue, and he's wearing his old, torn combat boots.

"Okay," I say. We've been talking about writing, which is what we always talk about.

"And I think we should always write what we want to, whether it sells or not," he says.

"Okay." This is easy for me because I can't imagine writing anything except what I want.

"We probably won't make a dime, you know. We'll probably starve."

"I know," I say, looking at the garden again.

I'm not worried.

It's July, 1993, and I'm visiting Gardner and Sue in Philadelphia. Gardner has become the foremost magazine editor in the field, which, in one sense, is my loss, for I can't drop a 200,000 word manuscript on his desk and ask him to edit it. He just doesn't have the time. Of course, in the old days I wasn't writing novels of that length. 1993 was a year of change for me, change and disruption . . . loss and gain.

It's 4:00 AM Gardner and I are sitting around in his living room.

"My career is down the tubes," I say. "I spent too much time on the da Vinci book. No one remembers who the hell I am."

"Then write me some short stories," Gardner says. "Christ, the readership changes every five years or so. If you want them to know who you are, get into the magazines."

I nod.

"Remember what I told you before?"

"What?" I ask.

"If you could go back to the early days and see yourself now, you'd think you'd died and gone to Heaven. You would have given anything to have a big book with Bantam and have your corpus of work . . . Well?"

"Yeah, I suppose."

But I had not expected to be in such pain.

However, I do have an idea for a new novel . . .

In 1975 I sold *Junction* to Gold Medal Books on the basis of an outline and about a hundred pages. I was living with Marcia, and we decided to move into one of my father's apartments. I remember working on *Junction* in my new study, which was the largest one I've ever had. It was filled with books, and the scuffed hardwood floor was covered with a worn oriental carpet purchased at a Salvation Army. Marcia was trying to become a dancer. She couldn't seem to hold down a job. She tried going back to college, but that didn't work out either. Money was once again tight, even with help from my family, and it was adversely affecting our relationship.

George Zebrowski suggested that I move into the building in which he and Pam Sargent were living. I looked at the apartment, which was quite spacious, and rented it. Although in retrospect it seemed like a crazy thing to do, I felt that new surroundings might help my relationship with Marcia; and I thought I would get more work done with George and Pam upstairs. Marcia and I had come to dislike the neighborhood we were living in, but I feel now that that was because we were having problems, and not because of the neighborhood.

So we moved into George and Pam's building in 1976, I believe, and broke up shortly thereafter. We continued seeing each other, but she finally moved to New York to pursue her career. Whether or not she is dancing, I don't know. But it was a difficult summer for me. I finished writing *Starhiker* as therapy. Gardner was still coming to visit, but not as much, as he was now living in Philadelphia with his girlfriend Susan Casper. Pam Sargent and I spent quite a bit of time together.

During that summer I became romantically involved with two women. One of them, Bev, had been a student of mine; the other Jeanne Carpenter, would later become my fiancé. I was trying to carry on two major relationships at the same time, and was living in a fool's paradise. But I was writing, and my story "The Dybbuk Dolls" was on the final ballot for the Nebula Award. That was enough reinforcement for me at the time.

Then I became blocked three quarters of the way through my novel *Junction*. I simply couldn't finish it. As I couldn't write, I read, walked around town late at night, and secluded myself. This went on for weeks, until one afternoon, after coming home from the park, I lay down for a nap. I had books spread all over the bed, books that I thought might help me over my block. I could hear George walking around in his bedroom upstairs, and then suddenly everything seemed to explode with light. I felt as if I were falling. (Of course, I was probably looking at the light bulb on the ceiling over my bed.) When I came out of this "episode", I knew the ending of the novel, down to the last physical and philosophical detail. I had a rough outline of the ending before, but I just couldn't make the external action fit into the internal set of the book.

I finished *Junction* in 1977, the same year that saw publication of *Starhiker*. My short stories were now beginning to be reprinted here and in Europe, and I sold a chapbook of poetry to Gil Williams of The Bellevue Press. A German publisher bought *Starhiker*. And my editor at Gold Medal was fired. He became my agent, and we negotiated with Gold Medal to buy back *Junction*. The new editor at Gold Medal told us they would publish the book, even though they felt it was too intellectual and wouldn't sell well. My agent thought it best to find a publisher who would get behind the book, and so *Junction* went on the market again.

But something dark was happening at home, had been happening and growing. I found myself at odds with George more and more of the time. Our relationship was deteriorating into something out of Strindberg's *The Ghost Sonata*, and I could only think of getting away from that red brick building on the north side of Johnson City.

But these two people were my family. Cutting off my relationship with them was like cutting out part of my life.

I bought a house on the south side of town. The house was cheap, and I could afford it, mortgage and all. The house, built in the 1860s, was very deteriorated, and one of my closest friends, Skip Radecker, who had worked for our family for over ten years, rebuilt it for me. He did that out of love, for I couldn't afford to pay him what he was worth.

While I was moving from my apartment to my new home, with boxes of books and clothes and bric-a-brac everywhere, I felt the old welling up of energy. I *had* to write. I propped my typewriter on some boxes and wrote in between trips to the house. The result was "Camps". The story was well received, widely reprinted, and was a finalist for the Nebula Award and the British Science Fiction Association Award. That was a watershed work for me. I had discovered a new control, a way of being both subjective and objective, a new voice that was outside the story but wouldn't distance the reader.

I moved into my house and, leaving it in disarray, left for the World Science Fiction Convention, which was being held in Miami, Florida. I rode with my friends Brian and Betsy Perry. It was two weeks out of time, or so it seems to me now.

I was free . . .

~

That was in the Fall of 1977. I would not feel that free until the Fall of 1993 at another Worldcon: the World Science Fiction Convention in San Francisco. There, at an author-editor party at Charlie Brown's in the California hills, I would step through a doorway and find myself in summer on the other side of the world.

~

In 1978 my professional life was doing quite well. I sold *Junction* to Dell and repaid Gold Medal their advance. I was beginning work on a novel that I had sold on outline to Harper & Row. My short story "A Quiet Revolution for Death" was being noticed and became a Nebula finalist. Several projects with Gardner were also in the works, but my personal life was a mess. I couldn't sustain my relationships with Jeanne and Bev. We were all miserable. I had let events take their course, but it had finally hit home how profoundly I was hurting two people I loved. I made the decision that summer, and shortly thereafter Jeanne and I decided to live together. I suddenly found myself with a family, for she had a son, Jody, who was six years old.

I spent the next year working on my novel for Harper, which I thought I would call *Amnesia*. I sold part of it to an anthology called *The Berkley Showcase*. And Gardner and I sold an anthology we had been working on entitled *Aliens!*. It was a quiet year. I felt good about family life and worked steadily. I was also spending quite a bit of time with Albert White, an Indian artist, who strongly influenced a work-in-progress called *Songs from a White Heart*, a series of poems.

It was with Albert that I thought I was going to catch on fire inside a sweat lodge. He was with me in the damp, burning dark when we felt the eagles beating and breathing like bellows. I wrote about that experience in *Counting Coup*. An excerpt entitled "Bad Medicine" was published in the October, 1984 issue of *Isaac Asimov's Science Fiction Magazine*. It became a Nebula finalist. I still find it difficult trying to explain that the most fantastical elements in the story were . . . real.

I sold a sequel to my first anthology, *Wandering Stars*, to Doubleday; and they published my short story collection, *Time-tipping*. Using some of the background from *The Man Who Melted*, I wrote "Going Under", a story about the resinking of the *Titanic*, and sold it to *Omni*. I was visiting Gardner often, although not quite as in the old days. But we were working! We wrote a novelette with a new author, Michael Swanwick, and sold it to *Penthouse*. We put together an anthology entitled *Unicorns!* and sold a story to *Playboy*. I was also doing collaborations with Barry Malzberg and Jack C. Haldeman II. I also changed my style, or stretched it, to write a comedy fantasy entitled "Fairy Tale". It's told in the first person by a stand-up comedian who discovers that leprechauns are taking over the borsht belt, and it became a World Fantasy Award finalist. Quite a change from "Amnesia" and "Camps". I think I wrote that story as a reaction to being called downbeat.

And in 1980 we discovered that Jeanne and Jody have a mild form of one of the muscular dystrophies called Charcot-Marie-Tooth disease. Decisions would have to be made, for Jeanne knew that she would eventually have to quit working as a nurse in the operating room and take a less physically demanding job. We went to Albert Einstein Hospital in New York City for another diagnosis. Barry Malzberg was there, sitting in the waiting room when we walked in.

He is certainly one of the *Lahmed Vov*, one of the Chosen.

～

February 20th, 1981. The present of things past:

And, as if coming to, I find myself back here in my office, tapping away at my blue Selectric. It's a cold sunny afternoon. My desk is covered with books, papers, and a photo of Jeanne and Jody. My radio is playing quietly. My coffee thermos is empty, and there are glass and ceramic miniature elephants scattered over my desk. They bring me luck, or so I superstitiously tell myself. If one must have a muse, it might as well be an elephant.

I've got to xerox some papers for Jeanne, for she has a scholarship to go back to college. I owe Barry a letter and am over deadline on several projects that need to be finished. I have two anthologies on the go, a treatment for a collaborative novel, and I'm dying to write *Counting Coup* and several short stories.

Thank God I'm still bursting with them.

All told, I must say, I've been lucky.

~

April 7th, 1994. The present of things present.

Thank God I couldn't see into the future. I'd have run for cover! And yet, as Gardner said, I would see many things to please me. The intervening years seem like a tunnel scattered with luminescent images. I've been as busy as I ever was, yet the busyness does not interest me as it once did; the recountings of stories and projects feel now like drudgery. Highlights will suffice.

But I was certainly right about one thing back in '81: I have been lucky. That luck was fraught with pain and anxiety and frustration . . . it's sad that learning to run with the daemons instead of fighting them takes most of a lifetime. I've finally learned to work without the constant internal injections of adrenaline.

Perhaps this diary might better have been called "Confessions of an Adrenaline Junkie".

~

Another present, July 18th, 2007, and, alas, I've been too often subject to self-delusion. I never really learned to work without those internal injections of adrenaline. (Right now I'm writing this autobiography against a tight deadline.) I tried, oh, how I tried, and perhaps I've discovered that the only daemon I might run with—or should run with—is myself.

All the others need to be wrestled down to the proverbial ground.

The biblical metaphor of Jacob wrestling with the angel—angel or daemon, one and the same—was spot-on for me because last year I discovered that I've always had a condition I thought was reserved for children: ADD, or Attention Deficit Disorder. I underwent a series of SPECT (single photon emission computed tomography) studies. Some of the tests were done while I was resting, others while I tried to solve problems on a computer. I could *see* what was wrong when I examined the SPECT scans: when I was resting, my brain looked like a normal brain at rest. However, when I concentrated, the activity in the underside and prefrontal cortex slowed right down. The more I tried to concentrate, the less activity was happening up there where I needed it.

Over the years I've developed techniques to ameliorate the problem. I learned how to slide into a resting, flow-like state. I became adept at various techniques of hypnosis, meditation, and lucid dreaming. I learned how to make the sharp transition from a relaxed state of mind to a state of hyperfocus. But I've spent a good part of my writing life trying to get there; it would often take hours for me to gain that state of mind where I could actually write. Once I'm writing, I'm actually quite fast.

I can't have all the lost time back; but with the help of some small dosages of meds, I can get to work without having to fool my brain that I'm really truly relaxing. I can go with the flow when I need to . . . but now I can also fight the sonovabitch daemons face to face.

Mostly I lose, of course.

So I'm rethinking how it all works, how I work; and when I'm writing and trying to find that precise descriptive word, it's good to be able to push through the dark and just grab it. Much better than having to wait . . . and wait . . . and wait.

Three cheers for adrenaline.

It's April, 1993, and I'm attending the I-Con convention in Stony Brook, New York. My wife Jeanne is not with me. I'm in the hotel bar with Lucius Shepard, who's living in Seattle. We don't get to see each other much any more.

"I've been wanting to talk to you for a long time, Jack," Lucius says. He leans close to me, this great, lovely, loving bull of a man, the same man who once drank a bottle of vodka and then asked my permission to pick up my refrigerator because he had just fallen in love. Lucius would have no trouble picking up refrigerators . . .

But then he grabbed me around the neck, squeezing me in a headlock, and he whispered, his face close to my ear, "Jack, you crazy, dumb sonovabitch, you're in deep water, and Jeanne is holding on to you—like this—because she's drowning. You can't breathe. You can't save her and yourself. What are you going to do?

"What are you going to do . . . ?"

In 1983, on New Year's Eve, Jeanne and I got married. I had proposed after returning from the funeral of my favorite cousin Mel Katz, who died in his early 50s. I had decided to lay down the sword and get on with life in a normal fashion. I was 38, and had never been married. In 1984 *The Man Who Melted* was published and was a Nebula finalist, as were three of the excerpts previously serialized as short stories. I was collaborating with Gardner and Michael Swanwick and Barry Malzberg, selling to the slicks such as *Penthouse*, *Playboy*, and *Omni*, and editing the *Magic Tales* series of fantasy anthologies with Gardner Dozois. These books include *Unicorns!*, *Magicats!*, *Bestiary!*, *Mermaids!*, *Sorcerers!*, *Demons!*, *Dogtails!*, *Seaserpents!*, *Dinosaurs!*, *Little People!*, *Magicats II!*, *Unicorns II!*, *Dragons!*, *Horses!*, *Invaders!*, *Angels!*, and *Dinosaurs II!*. The exclamation points were the publisher's idea! In 1987, Jeanne and I edited *In the Field of Fire*, a theme anthology about the Vietnam War; and it was the first science fiction anthology ever to receive a major, front page review by *The New York Times Book Review*. It was a finalist for the World Fantasy Award.

But money was still a constant problem.

I remember a six book series that fell through after the editor had told me that he was buying the books. I had begun spending the money on credit cards. One night, as I sat on my porch, a cable salesman tried to sell me Home Box Office. I needed money desperately, so I made a deal with him: if he would get me a job selling for the cable company, I would teach him how to write, for he was an aspiring writer. I had never sold anything in my life, but I discovered that I was quite good at it and found that by working four hours a night, I could make as much as the middle managers in the company. Later, I directed telemarketing and became a troubleshooter for the company, and when that wore thin, I became a sales manager for an insurance company.

Jeanne's illness was getting worse, and she knew she would not be able to continue as an operating room nurse. Jeanne went to college on scholarship, graduated magna cum laude, and received a scholarship to go on to graduate school. We had moved into a large house, and although Jeanne was on full scholarship, we needed more money.

But the hours at work took time away from my writing, and I began to live for week-ends; the weeks were drudgery, for once I had put a successful management system together, the rest was dull and pretty much pro forma. I was bored. I had begun researching Renaissance Italy, for I had an idea for a novel about the secret life of Leonardo da Vinci. I discussed the idea with Lou Aronica one Sunday over lunch in New York and sold the novel on the basis of enthusiasm and an outline.

It was more money than I had ever been paid for a book. I could quit my day job, which I did in 1988.

And a year after I quit, I was asked to become a director of the insurance company.

Sometimes it pays to be a writer . . .

~

But as the years passed, distance grew between Jeanne and me. Our relationship fell apart in small increments. The security of our home and Friday night Shabbat dinners had once attracted friends. We had been home and hearth, the golden couple. But we became angry and sullen. We argued in public, were silent alone.

Trust fell away.

We found ourselves signing separation and divorce agreements.

~

It's Fall, 1993. I've been attending the World Science Fiction Convention held in San Francisco. I'm riding on a bus with other Bantam authors; we're on our way to George Lucas's ranch. Bob Silverberg nods to me; we haven't seen each other in years. Although we rarely see each other, there has always been an intimacy to our meetings.

"I heard about you and Jeanne," Bob says.

I nod.

"I remember the two of you when my marriage was ending. You two looked so secure. Everything was in place for you, and everything was falling apart for me. Now the tables have turned." He looks at me with a knowing look that is Bob's alone. We smile, and he returns to his seat next to his new wife. Indeed, he looks happy.

~

But the winds of change were already sweeping me away. Hours later, I would fall in love. At first sight. If I had not been struck squarely in the heart by the archetype, I would never have believed it.

I met Janeen Webb, and a few months later became an expatriate. She said it best in a fax dated September 11, 1993:

We met at full moon, on a night of transition—neither summer nor autumn; we met in a doorway on a deck over woodland—neither inside nor outside, neither wild nor domestic, neither on the ground nor in the air—a door into faery; we were both jetlagged—neither waking nor sleeping; and both at a party—neither dining nor fasting, neither drunken nor sober; we were open to magic, and true recognition—the threshold was crossed before we were even aware.

~

And this finishes it for this present of things present. Right now I'm doing research for *The Silent* and working with Jack C. Haldeman on the sequel to our novel *High Steel*, which was published in 1993 and well received.

The future will certainly be its own master and have at me in ways I'd rather not know. In the meantime, I'll live every precious minute with all the juice and energy and joy I can muster.

~

Back to the (present of things) future . . .

Every moment has become more precious now that the shadows of mortality grow larger and larger, spreading slowly but inexorably across previously sunlit plains and paddocks. Yes, the future did have at me. It's all been surprises, moments of calm, terror, epiphany, grace, and joy. Successes and failures. All the little arcs and secants, the risings and restings and fallings of every little life.

1994, and the *Magic Tales* anthologies that I had been editing with Gardner continued to appear like clockwork. I also continued to write short stories, solo and in collaboration with Barry Malzberg and with Gardner Dozois. *High Steel* was published in hard covers and serialized in *Amazing*—a novella, "Echoes of Thunder" was also published as part of the Tor Doubles series. Jay and I would soon sell *Ghost Dance*, the sequel to *High Steel*, on the basis of a five page outline; I would also sell *The Silent* on outline. But I was spending almost all of my time working on *The Memory Cathedral*. It took six years to complete. I finished it days before I left for Australia. I had escaped into my world of the Renaissance during the difficult days and months of separating from Jeanne. It was my lifeline.

I remember talking to my agent Merrilee Heifetz in 1995, just before I left Melbourne for a quick business trip to Binghamton and New York. Merrilee told me that an auction situation had developed in Germany for *The Memory Cathedral*.

"But don't get your hopes up, Jack. The usual advance is 5,000 DM."

Indeed, it was; but when I reached Binghamton, there were about five messages from Merrilee. It had been a serious auction . . . for serious money.

The book became a bestseller in Germany and Australia, but I had moved away from that fertile historical period and was involved with a completely different kind of novel, a novel about a boy caught up in the Civil War.

I tried writing *The Silent* from an omniscient observer's point of view, but I couldn't get my young protagonist's voice out of my head. Edmund "Mundy" McDowell seemed to be continually whispering to me, telling me his story directly; and I realized

71

that I would have to write his story . . . from *his* point of view and in his voice. In fact, the opening of the book came to me while I was writing the third chapter. I suddenly stopped what I was doing because I heard Mundy "whispering" in the background; I shifted to a new screen to "transcribe" what he said. It was like automatic writing:

I wrote this, and then Uncle Randolph went over it and fixed my sentences and punctuation and broke everything up into sections and put in some of the quotations and fixed whatever else could be fixed. Uncle Randolph and Doctor Keys think it's "therapeutical" for me to write down what happened. They think if I can just write about all the terrible things that happened, they'll sort of go away or something and I won't think they were all my fault.

I think that Uncle Randolph shouldn't listen to doctors.

Anyway, I tried to write like everybody talked, but with some of the colored dialect it was hard to write it down, so I just did the best I could. Uncle Randolph went over that too. And he took out some of the swear words, which he said wouldn't read well because he said I had too many of them, but he left some in so you could get a feel for the truth. He didn't take out anything important, though, even though he said it made his heart sick to read it.

I don't know about that.

It's done now, and if anything's wrong it's probably my fault.

Anyway, it's mostly true.

—Edmund "Mundy" McDowell
November 16, 1864
Scranton, Pennsylvania

When I wrote "Scranton, Pennsylvania", I sat and stared at the words, wondering . . . The entire novel was supposed to take place in Virginia, in the Shenandoah Valley. What the hell was going on? I've learned that when the characters start telling me things, I listen. Just as my characters forced a fifty page exorcism scene into *The Memory Cathedral*, so would I have to figure out how and why Mundy ended up in Scranton, Lord help him.

Yes, I suppose there is something a bit schizophrenic about this writing business. Perhaps that's why I took a tip from Peter Straub and always suit up when doing business. The idea is to *try* to look normal!

I married Janeen Webb on June 17th, 1995 and we traveled extensively in the States, lecturing and researching *The Silent*. My old friend and mentor Roger Zelazny died. My novella "Da Vinci Rising", which I adapted from *The Memory Cathedral*, was the cover story for the May issue of *Asimov's* and won a Nebula Award. Keith Ferrell and Ellen Datlow commissioned another novella to launch *Omni*'s on-line *Neon/Visions* publishing venture. "Jubilee" was later included in a large, retrospective collection of my short fiction, which I titled . . . *Jubilee*. *The Memory Cathedral* was published in a limited leather-bound first edition by The Easton Press and in a general hardcover edition by Bantam Press. It won the Aurealis Award and was shortlisted for the Ditmar Award, the British Fantasy Award, and the Benalla Award for the Audio Book of the Year. Janeen and I wrote an article for *Omni* about Lawrence Hargrave, the Australian inventor of the box kite; and after a disastrous visit to Niagara Falls in 1996 (Go and see the Falls, but for goodness sake, don't stay there!), we wrote a story for *Japanese Futures*, edited by Keith Ferrell and Orson Scott Card, called "Niagara Falling". Janeen and I don't collaborate easily; being married and having strong personalities has evidently charged our work, for "Niagara Falling" won both the Aurealis and Ditmar Awards in 1997 and was reprinted in three best of the year collections. We went on to edit *Dreaming Down-Under*, a collection of original Australian science fiction, fantasy, and horror. It was the first Australian volume ever to win a World Fantasy Award.

I did quite a bit of editing while I was writing *The Silent*. Besides *Dreaming*, I edited a number of volumes in the *Magic Tales* series with Gardner: *Hackers, Timegates, Clones, Immortals, Nanotech, Future War*, and *Armageddons*. I also edited the collections of classic novels *Three In Time* and *Three In Space* with Pamela Sargent and George Zebrowski. We had planned on doing an entire series of what we considered enduring classics for new readers, but the publisher, White Wolf, alas, folded. We did manage to bring back into print *The Winds of Time* by Chad Oliver, *The Year of the Quiet Sun* by Wilson Tucker, *There Will Be Time* and *The Enemy Stars* by Poul Anderson, *Voyage of the Space Beagle* by A. E. van Vogt, and *Galaxies* by Barry N. Malzberg. I also edited the thirty-second Nebula Awards anthology for the Science Fiction Writers of America.

In 1996 I became a consulting editor for Tor and was able to bring Australian authors Sean McMullen and Paul Brandon into print in America. I was also doing a number of guest-of-honor gigs and various public speaking engagements.

Unfortunately, I was not a confident speaker.

I remember reading a paper on *The Memory Cathedral* at the Powerhouse Museum in Sydney. Harlan Ellison, Terry Dowling, artist Nick Stathopoulos, and I were the special guests of a conference. (It was basically the Harlan Ellison convention.) After I read the paper, Harlan, who dutifully sat and listened for the full hour—because that's what you do for family—came up to the podium and said: "Jack, why the hell did you have to read all that? Why didn't you just talk about the book? You know more about it than anyone else."

I blinked and said, "I needed a net in case I drew a complete blank."

Harlan looked at me like I was a four-headed, weak-brained, twelve-tentacled alien from Deneb and said, "The audience isn't interested in listening to you read a prepared speech. They want a piece of *you*. They want to see into *you*. The whole point is to work without a net."

I blinked again. What the hell could I say to that . . . ?

~

It's August, 1998, and I'm a guest of the Melbourne Writers' Festival. I've been invited to speak on a panel called "Writers and Mathematics".

Go figure. I consider geometry, trigonometry, Boolean algebra, and negative numbers to be in the same category as trying to spell words such as "antidisestablishmentarianism", comprehending concepts such as the measurement of infinities, Jacques Derrida's linguistics and grammatology, and visualizing a trillion dollars neatly stacked in rows. But my publisher has managed to get me a gig at the festival, which was no easy task. My job is to try to sound intelligent, crack a joke, and promote my books. After all, this is just a *panel*. I've done hundreds of panels at science fiction conventions. The moderator introduces the panelists, asks a question, and everyone has a discussion. It's like schmoozing in front of an audience. That I don't know squat about math shouldn't be a problem. I'll make a few pithy remarks, nod sagely, and try to get through the hour.

To my right sits Diane Armstrong, author of the brilliant *Mosaic: A Chronicle of Five Generations*, which was acclaimed by the late Joseph Heller and Nobel prizewinner Elie Wiesel. To my left sits Sue Woolfe, author of *Leaning Towards Infinity*, a novel about a housewife who happens to be a mathematical genius. *Leaning Towards Infinity* is one of my favorite Australian novels.

75

Diane leans over to me and asks, "What the hell are we doing here?"

I grin and shrug. Well, at least Sue is right on target for this panel, as are the two other mathematically oriented writers, one of whom is the moderator. The moderator stands up, sidles over to the podium, adjusts the microphone, and proceeds to read a rigorous paper on the interrelations of writing and mathematics. Then he announces the next panelist, who stands up to the podium, paper in hand, and reads to the audience.

I'm totally screwed. Here I am on a panel about a subject I know nothing about, and I certainly don't have a rigorous paper to give. If I had known what the Melbourne Writers' Festival required, I might have cribbed something from "The Aerodynamics of a Strapless Evening Gown".

There is nothing for me to do now but listen to the others and pray to the gods of atheists that I won't be next. Sue reads her paper, which is wonderful. Diane reads her paper about the Holocaust and her family, and the audience is in tears.

Then someone else reads, reads in a monotone, and I discover that even in this state of vague yet embracing terror, I have become dozy and sleepy. The audience and I have entered a complementary state of drowsy, nodding harmony, but for my vague awareness that soon I will be in writer's hell; and then—cruelly pulled away from the strong and comforting arms of Morpheus—I realize with a start that the moderator is introducing someone called Jack Dann who has written something called *The Memory Cathedral*.

The moderator motions me up to the podium and apologizes that, alas, this panel is in danger of exceeding its time limit, and Jack Dann won't have the proper amount of time to read his paper.

Perhaps there *is* a God!

I get up, in slow motion . . .

Well, Harlan, I might as well give them a piece of me. I sure as hell don't have anything mathematically brilliant to add to this convocation . . . and I don't have anything to lose. Screw it. The worst the audience can do is kill me; and, suddenly, I find myself in this odd state of consciousness, somewhere between that alpha state of flow that enables me to write and a vertiginous sense of doubleness, as if I'm watching myself from a safe distance.

I start to talk, summarizing what everyone else has said, trying to make sense of the subject; and then I'm somehow telling jokes and the audience . . . I can see the audience *waking up*. They're smiling, nodding; this is a conversation, one on one, and suddenly I feel like I'm in my salad days, that it's all sex, drugs, and rock n' roll all over again, and the gray haired eminence of Australia, well, that sumbitch is . . . *cookin'*!

I've just discovered stand-up.

I sit down and Diane asks, "How the hell do you do *that*?"

I grin, bewildered, and whisper, "Thanks, Harlan . . . "

After that Melbourne Writers' Festival, I found myself doing a lot of public speaking. It became as natural as chatting with friends, and I'm usually surprised by what I end up telling the audience. If I had known all those years ago that public speaking was, in certain respects, like writing, I wouldn't have pretended to be the *artiste* who scorns crowds. But public life sucks up more and more time. Less writing gets done. So right now in this future of 2007, Mr. Stand-Up is bit by bit, hour by hour, week by week transmogrifying himself back into an *artiste* hermit so he can get his work done before he and his attendant mortal coil are thrown headlong off the speeding, paint-faded bus . . .

And in those fanciful dreams that I so desperately wish I could buy into, I'd spend an eternity hanging around in Writers' Heaven with Jay Haldeman, Roger Zelazny, Bob Sheckley, Don Klisto, Pete McNamara, Norman Talbot, Rich Alverson, Alfie

Bester, Damon Knight, John Ford, George Alec Effinger, and sweet Jenna Felice.

∽

The Silent was published in the US in 1998. Reviewers loved it. Reviewers hated it. This business of pushing the envelope, writing the work I needed to write, could be quite dangerous . . . and exhilarating. *The Silent* was one of *Library Journal*'s "Hot Picks": "From the author of *The Memory Cathedral*, this is narrative story-telling at its best—so highly charged emotionally as to constitute a kind of poetry from hell. Most emphatically recommended."

British critic John Clute wrote, "In some ways, *The Silent* resembles Jerzy Kosinski's *The Painted Bird* (1965), which is set in peneplainal apocalyptic Poland during World War Two, and which also features a young boy who has been driven mute by his experiences. But it's *The Painted Bird* as told by Huckleberry Finn. Mundy's narrative has the twist and muscle and flow . . . of Twain's rendering of Finn's serio-comic spelunking into the Darklands of America; but Mundy's odyssey is into the dreamwork of hell."

But *Publishers Weekly* wrote: "Dann's maudlin but sporadically engaging second novel (after *The Memory Cathedral*) treats the Civil War as a phantasmagoric experience and takes the form of a 'therapeutical' memoir set down (in 1864!) by 13-year-old Virginian Edmund McDowell . . . The account is burdened by the repetitive, ill-defined symbolism of a 'spirit dog', the ghost of a slave named 'Jimmadasin' and an enigmatic icon known as 'baby Jesus'. Innuendoes—that the famously rigid, religious Gen. Stonewall Jackson tipples on the side, and that McDowell's hero, Col. Ashby, is a pedophile—lend the tale neither depth nor veri-similitude . . . No number of rapes and pillagings can bring this tedious, ahistorical novel to life."

When the novel was published in Australia the following year, it received enthusiastic, full-page reviews in all the major newspapers. The reviewer for *The Australian* said, "Tough, allusive, engaging and revealing, it has a magical realist edge yet is more real than most history texts . . . *The Silent* is an extraordinary achievement."

The praise was reinforcing, intoxicating, exhilarating, inspiring, but the next time I set about smashing treasured icons, I would find the reception enthusiastic, angry, savage, or resoundingly silent.

~

June, 1974, and I'm standing in the converted barn of Francois Bucher, a Swiss art historian living in upstate New York. Picture windows overlook rolling hills, the ceiling is glass laid over timber; the walls are covered with expressionist paintings and cubist prints, and there are prints and sculptures and ancient artifacts and book-thick piles of paper scattered and piled along the edges of the floor: obstacles that form the perimeters of his one great sleeping-eating-working-entertaining-living room. I've been invited to "maybe do some business".

I'm twenty-nine years old, still a hustling-hoping-somehow-to-get-to-my-next-meal free-lance writer, and Bucher has invited me to meet Nicholas Ray, the iconic director of *They Live by Night*, *Johnny Guitar*, *The Lusty Men*, *55 Days at Peking*, and the film that turned James Dean into a legend: *Rebel without a Cause*.

Francois introduces me to Nick Ray. I feel awkward, and then suddenly I'm calm and cool and focused and I don't give a rat's ass what happens because immediately and without a blink, Nick Ray and I are playing the game. We're facing each other like combatants. Staring hard at each other. Not saying a word. For a few hot seconds, I *am* James Dean; and so is Nick. He's just playing an older version of James Dean: himself. We're both wearing jeans and tee shirts. All that's missing is Dean's emblematic red jacket. Nick is my size, with a shock of curly white hair, a lined and rugged face, and a black patch like a pirate's over his right eye. He makes the first move and tells me he's working on a new film, asks me if I'd like to look at the rushes.

I nod.

We're having a wonderful time . . .

June, 1997, and I'm standing on the balcony of my suite on the eighth floor of The Beverly Prescott Hotel in Beverly Hills. I gaze down Pico Boulevard as the Mercs and BMW's and Rollers glide silently by below. Beside me stands Patsy LoBrutto, my dear friend of over twenty years and now my editor for *The Silent*. We've taken a day here in LA to edit the novel, which is finished, and then both of us will travel to the Hotel Queen Mary (once a grand ship that took me to Southampton) where we're guests at a convention.

While a hot wind gentles around us (it's winter in Melbourne, Australia, and I'm glad to be here, glad for the heat), Patsy and I stand on that balcony and look out at the shimmering urban sprawl where the American Dream is manufactured and packaged and polished, and we discuss possible projects. I reel off idea after idea. Pat looks glum and shakes his head. "They're lovely, but they're not going to capture that audience." He nods at the shimmering offices and apartment buildings in the distance. He doesn't have to point; I know what he means.

"What's your favorite movie?"

I shrug, and Frank Capra's 1937 *Lost Horizon* starring Ronald Colman comes to mind. So I blurt it out, but already I'm thinking of Nick's *Rebel without a Cause*—*Lost Horizon* for its magic, *Rebel without a Cause* because of James Dean.

And I remember standing in Francois Bucher's barn with Nick Ray, remember driving flat-out with Nick over country roads during that sweaty, compressed, juicy journey of my youth. Dammit, Nick, I knew then that we'd play James Dean again. Only this time I won't be looking at the rushes. I'll be "writing" them.

And there, in that instant, it seems perfectly natural to conflate the magical realism of *Lost Horizon* with the "long and legendary" life of James Dean.

"Dean doesn't die in the accident, Patsy. I'm going to tell the *real* story about James Dean . . . what happens after his accident."

I can see it, not yet clearly; but as well as I can see the buildings in the hazed distance.

And so in 1997, I began the research for *Second Chance*, a novel that would be published in 2004 as *The Rebel: An Imagined Life of James Dean*. I wanted to write an iconography of American politics and popular culture. I wanted to get inside the heads of Marilyn Monroe, James Dean, Robert F. Kennedy, Jack Kerouac, Elvis Presley, JFK, LBJ, Frank Sinatra, Joe DiMaggio, and William Burroughs. I wanted to write my own honky-tonk, drug-soaked, rock n'roll, true-to-the-essence of life, larger-than-life, sweet sad tragic violent insecure ambitious jubilant millennial-optimistic all-American *Dance to the Music of Time*. I wanted to immerse myself so deeply in the period that I could see into and through the icons, read their thoughts, deeds, yearnings, miseries, joys—their very lives—and transcribe them into a *true* history, a history that didn't quite happen, a history that would reveal our past and those who created it and were caught up in it. I wanted to alter the past only slightly, just inject a bit of dye into it, as if I were running a SPECT scan. I wanted to irradiate the truth we imagine to know so well. I wanted to reveal who and what we were and might have been by simultaneously charting what was *and* what might have been. And so I read primary and secondary sources, and mined my own memories, for I had been privileged to sit in the smoke-filled rooms, had known some of the key political players, had been pulled along on that wild wagon of the 60s and 70s . . . and had my phone tapped, apartment ransacked, did the drugs, sang the songs, decided not to go to West Point or join the FBI, went to law school, remained a Republican, met Timothy Leary, tuned in, dropped out, then dropped back in again once and for all (not, I might mention, as a Republican).

While I researched, dreamed, and remembered the America of my past, I lived and worked. I edited anthologies, wrote stories, had small epiphanies and aches and pains, made mistakes, tried to fix mistakes, kept in touch with friends all over the world by phone and e-mail, got involved in film, moved to the farm overlooking the sea, made new friends and discovered new enemies, bought an apartment in Melbourne, cried in the car with my brother Lorne after saying goodbye to my dying Mother in a nursing home in Birmingham, Alabama, played the stock market, decided not to dye my shock of white (no longer gray) hair or get a hair transplant or a nip-and-a-tuck face lift, and fought the daily fight against the daily dying of the light.

My road novel *Counting Coup* was published in Australia (as *Bad Medicine*) in 2000 and in the US in 2001. It had quite a history: I wrote it in 1985, after spending a year of research with a young Native American medicine man. I sold the book to Bluejay Books in 1986 . . . and then Bluejay folded. As the years passed, the manuscript became dog-eared, agents became frustrated, and the novel began to develop a reputation as an unpublished samizdat classic. In 1996 White Wolf Books contracted to publish the book . . . then White Wolf folded.

It took another four years, but the curse finally lifted; and in my afterword to the Australian edition I wrote:

My characters often have different "intentions" than their author, who often sits bemusedly in front of the laptop while the characters engage in their own conversations and take the "plot" in directions I never intended. I had intended *Bad Medicine* to be a straight-forward road novel, a novel about two men who are at the end of their lives and decide to show the world that they are still alive, still vital, and can still drink, shout, and shake the trees. I thought I'd write a novel in the tradition of Jack Kerouac's *On the Road*, or John Steinbeck's *Cannery Row*. Originally, I thought it would be interesting to explore the interaction of two men from different cultures in similar circumstances. But once again the research changed the story . . . and of course my life.

The elements of magical realism in *Counting Coup* are close to the truth of my own private experiences. I have found as I enter my more mature, reflective years that my "real" life is scattered with these small bits of magic realism. Or perhaps it's just that as I wander through that distant country that is my past I recast the ordinary into the numinal.

For me fiction has always been a way of ordering and remembering experience; and I came closest to remembering the sight and smell and "feel" of those experiences when I wrote *Counting Coup*. Once again I could hear the spirit voices and feel the steam that's so hot it's cold. Once again I remembered what happened when everything soured and turned into "bad medicine".

Once again I remembered being on the road, living without impediment . . .

And once again my fiction and my personal life blurred, one folding into the other.

The *Magic Tales* volumes edited with Gardner continued to appear: *Aliens Among Us*, *Genometry*, *Space Soldiers*, *Future Sports*,

Beyond Flesh, Future Crimes, A.I's. In collaboration with Grania Davis, I edited an edition of Avram Davidson's short stories entitled *Everybody Has Somebody in Heaven: Essential Jewish Tales of the Spirit.* My retrospective short story collection *Jubilee* was published in 2002, followed by *Visitations*, another short story collection, in 2003. I was also editing an original collection of dark fantasy and horror called *Gathering the Bones* with Ramsey Campbell and Dennis Etchison. Our subtitle—never used—was *Tales of Terror from Three Continents*, which pretty well summed up our intentions for the book. I had a not-so-hidden agenda: after *Dreaming Down-Under*, I wanted another chance to show-case the talent of Australian genre writers such as Terry Dowling, Isobelle Carmody, Rosaleen Love, Janeen Webb, and Simon Brown. And while I was editing anthologies, living with James Dean and Elvis Presley, Marilyn Monroe, and Bobby Kennedy in the 1960s—and Janeen Webb in those last years of the twentieth century and first years of the twenty-first—I continued to write stories: "Blind Eye", "Ships" with Michael Swanwick, "Niagara Falling" and "The Fire-Eater's Tale" with Janeen, "Marilyn" (also turned into a radio play for Scifi.com), "Ting-a-Ling", "The Hanging", "Summer", "The Starry Night" with Barry Malzberg, "The Diamond Pit", and handfuls of other stories.

"The Diamond Pit" was my homage to F. Scott Fitzgerald, "A Diamond As Big as the Ritz" told from the point of view of a pilot held prisoner by the richest man on earth. It was great fun to write. It won the Australian Ditmar Award and was shortlisted for the Aurealis, Nebula, and Hugo awards. I was working, writing every day, spending the collapsing hours in my darkened studio, dreaming and writing *The Rebel*. But there were faint shadows lengthening on the horizon, hints of "bad medicine", bad juju, some physical illness (I have not mentioned that Janeen had been very ill), and some "business" trouble. I learned once again that there are people out there who want a piece of you—and your work—and some of them have their own surgeons (silks, solici-

84

tors, lawyers) ready and willing to operate. I learned the hard way and obtained my own surgeons. Now, I don't do very much without checking with solicitors, agents, accountants, and financial planners.

So much for the life of the *artiste* . . .

While I was writing *The Rebel*, my film agent and dear friend, kept nagging me to get a DVD of *Wonder Boys*, starring Michael Douglas. It's about a writer working on a novel that never ends. I was in grave danger of doing the same, for *The Rebel* had come to life; and I was typing as fast as I could to capture the smells, emotions, light, darkness, and the very "thickness" of its sum and substance. But I did finish it in 2003. Although I had contracted for a 100,000 word novel, I had written over 280,000 words . . . over eleven hundred pages. Writing turned into the painful left-brained analytical business of editing, condensing, revising, and cutting. If there is such a thing as Editors' Heaven, my editors Jennifer Brehl and Linda Funnell are certainly assured of mansions the size of Versailles.

The novel was published in 2004, and I remember making the long-haul flight to LA on a Qantas jet. Some 30,000 feet in the air, I pulled on headphones and clicked the dial on the moveable armrest through the audio channels and stopped when I heard Harlan holding forth on literature and critics . . . only it wasn't Harlan. With a distinct shock I realized that I was listening to my own insistent, snapping twanging voice. I had done an interview with Qantas Airlines months ago. How could I have forgotten, as the technician in the sound studio had inadvertently turned the volume control on my earphones to maximum. When the interviewer came on the line, I almost fell off the chair. My ears rang like Big Ben for the rest of the day. The interviewer asked me about the perils of messing with people's icons, something akin to messing with dreams and hopes. Without missing a beat, I said that the writer's business is to write the books that have to be written. If what I write upsets critics, that's their problem.

85

Well, it's only *their* problem if the writer is independently wealthy, egoless, saintly, or one of Leibnitz's happy and harmonious windowless monads.

Reviewers loved the book. Reviewers hated the book. A few mainstream reviewers couldn't get past the idea that James Dean survived the accident. *But he died!* A few genre reviewers considered it a mainstream novel. More than a few reviewers were indignant. One wrote that I hadn't done any research at all, and her proof was that I had described Elvis Presley as having blond hair. The only problem I had with her keen analysis was that Elvis *did* have blond hair; he dyed it black. Another castigated the author for allowing the characters too many swear words. *Kirkus* called it "a Harold Robbins-style tale of gratuitous sex, ambition, and famous people behaving badly . . . Relentlessly trashy and profane, name-dropping and scandal-mongering". When I read the *Kirkus* review to my film agent, she thought it was wonderful, which sort of brings the business into proper perspective.

And, of course, there were the grand reviews: "Dann's carefully crafted novel builds up to a stunning climax, and contains several beautifully written erotic scenes. Dann is justly famed for the depth and quality of the research he brings to his novels, and in this case, he's helped by having done more than that: he habituated the coffee houses in the years of the beats and the beehive hairdo, hung out with hippies in the 60s, met Timothy Leary and worked with Nick Ray, and became involved in American politics in the 80s and 90s. This has enabled him to create an amazingly evocative and utterly convincing picture of the era, down to details of the smells and sensations—and even more importantly, the way of thinking . . . *The Rebel's* greatest triumph lies in its characterization—particularly its portrayal of Marilyn Monroe, Robert Kennedy, and James Dean himself, all three of them apparently godlike, but internally fallible and utterly human . . . "

Or this, from *Locus*, a genre insiders' magazine: "Dann limns the psychology of conflicted inspiration as brilliantly as he did in his major novel of ten years ago, *The Memory Cathedral*, wherein he considered another troubled bisexual genius, Leonardo da Vinci. But where that treatment was ornate, mannered, painterly, *The Rebel* is plainspoken, graphic, dominated by clipped, blunt dialogue in place of elaborate description and formal colloquy. Jimmy's personal discussions and confrontations, often by phone, possess a crackling laconic energy worthy of a powerful film script. In this Dann has embraced a technique perfect for a Hollywood psychological novel, and it is by his words, tender or frenzied, that the phantom of James Dean acquires full, extraordinary life. No superficial Tinseltown gossip here, no languorous intrigues on the film set: instead, private torment, public rage . . . "

And on and on, but I was focused on those encroaching dark shadows, living with lawyers and accountants, and wrestling with ideas for new novels. I'd become impatient. I didn't want to wait for the next big novel to find me. I was too old to be passive. I was busily proactive. I sold a collection of my collaborative stories and called it *The Fiction Factory*. Gardner and I edited more *Magic Tales* volumes— *Robots, Beyond Singularity, Futures Past*—as well as two young adult original collections: *Escape From Earth* and *Wizards* (titled *Dark Alchemy* in Great Britain). I edited another Nebula Awards volume, *Nebula Awards® Showcase 2005* and *Dreaming Again*, the sequel to *Dreaming Down-Under*, which will be published in 2008. And still the short stories appeared: "Rings Around the Moon", "Good Deeds", "Bugs", "Dreaming with the Angels", "The Starry Night" and "Faulkner's Seesaw" with Barry Malzberg, "Promised Land", "River" with Keith Ferrell, "The Method", "King of the Mountain", and the political "Café Culture", which carried a reader's warning in the January 2007 issue of *Asimov's Magazine*. My British publisher asked if I would consider doing a collection of my James Dean stories, and so I sold a companion volume to *The Rebel* called *Promised Land: Stories of Another America*.

In his gracious and rigorous introduction to the collection, Kim Stanley Robinson synthesizes exactly what I was trying to do with this material:

> Dann presents his fictional world through the lens of the celebrities with whom James Dean was associating at the time of his death, augmented by some of those he might have met if he had lived. The cast of characters is therefore eye-popping: the Kennedys and their crowd, Elvis Presley and his crowd, Marilyn Monroe and her crowd. This is a good part of the pantheon of mid-Twentieth century American culture gods, and so one of the things going on in this collection is a different kind of "what if" than that presented in the usual alternative history: not only "what if James Dean had lived?" but also, and perhaps more importantly for this particular collection: "what if most of the myths we tell about that generation of celebrities were based on truths?" This is another kind of fictional idea generator, a kind of archeology of narrative, which says: If the myths and rumors about these people were based on real events, refracted through the lens of retellings, what would have had to have happened, back at the beginning, in order to create the material for us to spin out those myths and rumors? Regarding only the various clouds and columns of smoke, can one then present to the reader the fire itself?

I started intensive research on a novel about Niccolo Machiavelli. I plotted out my military school novel *Extra Duty* as a psychological, political thriller. I was guest of honor at Dragoncon in Atlanta, Georgia, a convention of over 30,000 people who came together in fabulous costumes and Hollywood make-up to create a small city, an enormous party of writers, producers, actors, and fans, a *Star Wars* bar-scene version of Woodstock. I searched for that numinal, glowing idea that would bloom into the next novel I *had* to write . . . and the voices stopped whispering, the "little man" inside my head stopped *noodjing* me: a bad sign when your very own unconscious gives up on you. So I stopped trying to be proactive, stopped trying to pretend to be an adult, the white-haired eminence of Australia, and went back to being a curious, joyful, immature, dancing bear of a man-child hermit reader writer observer "with blue eyes magnified to the size of eggs". (Kim Stanley Robinson's eye-catching description of my stunned-mullet persona.) Once again, I heard the faint whispering . . . once again the little man started bossing me around, and I found myself collaborating with one of my past selves on a short novel entitled *The Economy of Light*, a story I had started twenty years ago, but just couldn't finish . . . until now. The ending had always been right there, as obvious as a doorway into summer. I just needed older eyes to see it. As Michael Swanwick wrote in his introduction to the novella: "Perhaps, just as there are certain books you have to grow into as a reader, this was one he had to grow into as a writer."

And I'm writing *Ghost Dance*, the sequel to *High Steel*, with Barbara Delaplace, Jay Haldeman's partner.

Jay, my traveling friend, who truly exists in my conflation of a heaven for the disbeliever, it's as if you're right here in the room.

So now I'm all growed up. I remember calling my father "the world's oldest adolescent". He was quite indignant at what he considered to be a profound slur.

No, Dad, it wasn't a slur.

It was your greatest gift to your wayward son . . . inheritance is a wonderful thing.

~

July 27th, 2007. I call Gardner. He's back home from his operation and complaining that he can't settle back into work quickly enough. I'm relieved; he won't be getting off the bus anytime soon. He tells me that he's heard that our YA anthology *Wizards* is Number 8 on the Waldenbooks/Borders hardcover bestseller list.

Hooray . . . maybe, if it's true.

Let's do another book, fellow bus traveler.

And I'm sorting out those pesky voices. Once again, a new novel calls to me, irritates me, pulls my slippered thoughts away from the lush winter garden outside the window, away from friends, airport novels, stock market fluctuations, and into those dark, dark places where magic still shelters . . .

Windhover Farm
South Gippsland
Victoria, Australia
28 July 2007

Seasons Greetings
1962
The Danns